CONTENTS

Introduction: Reading the Difference

Myra Barrs

The topic of gender and reading is littered with unresolved paradoxes. Prime among these is the fact that although there is widespread and longstanding acknowledgement of differences existing between girls and boys, and men and women, as readers, there has been remarkably little serious discussion of issues of gender in relation to the teaching and learning of reading.

The main differences between girls and boys as readers that are generally recognised but rarely talked about are three. One is the fact that girls read more than boys. A long succession of reading surveys, from Jenkinson's *What do Boys and Girls Read?* in 1940 to Whitehead's *Children and their Books* in 1977, have shown that sex is the major factor in studies of children as readers, being more strongly linked than either social class or ability and attainment with how much children read. Leng's study *Children in the Library* (1968) found that the most important differentiating factor was that of sex, since "the bulk of children who join are girls and the majority of those who abstain are boys". Whitehead reports that "At all ages girls read more than boys, and at the same time there are fewer non-book readers among the girls than among the boys".

The second difference relates to the *content* of boys' and girls' reading. Again, reading surveys of both children and adults for many years have regularly pointed to the fact that females and males choose to read different kinds of material and different types of fiction. Thorndike's *Comparative Study of Children's Reading Interests* (1941), for instance, found that there was a consistent pattern of boy-interests and girl-interests in children's choices, which cut across all age and intelligence differences in his sample. Sex was conspicuously the most important determinant of reading interest patterns. Later surveys have shown the same marked differences, and the adult reading index repeatedly confirms that females read more fiction than males, while males read more non-fiction than females. Teachers recognise these same patterns to be characteristic of girls' and boys' reading interests and choices in classrooms.

The third difference is in the area of *achievement*. It is generally known that girls consistently achieve more highly than boys in reading. Girls' higher attainment is regularly reflected in reading test results and SATs results, as well as in children's achievement on other measures such as the Primary Language Record reading scales (Feeney and Hann, 1991). The recent OFSTED report on *Boys and English* shows that girls do better than boys in reading and writing at all ages, and that this is reflected in public examination results. This difference is so much a part of conventional wisdom that allowance is made for it in the scoring systems of many reading tests. Girls' scores are frequently adjusted downwards when test results are calculated, to make up for the difference between girls and boys. The reasoning behind this adjustment goes back to the time of the 11 plus examination, and to the fact that girls were thought to develop more rapidly than boys at about this age, mentally as well as physically. They were therefore handicapped in order to ensure that they did not out-perform the boys and monopolise the limited grammar school places available because of a developmental anomaly.

It seems that the differences between girls and boys as readers are well attested, a part of common knowledge. One reason they may engender so little discussion in educational circles is because they have taken on the character of truisms; they are regarded as unproblematic facts. Yet such marked differences between groups of children, particularly differences in the area of achievement, would not be so readily accepted if the groups were defined by class, race, or language background. Perhaps we need to 'problematise' a little the long-accepted differences between boys and girls as readers. A habit of thinking about equal opportunities makes it harder to ignore such differences, or to regard them as 'natural' or 'innate'. Recently, teachers and educationalists have begun to explore some of the tangled and difficult questions surrounding the topic of gender and reading, and to look seriously at the possibility that low attainment in certain areas is being perpetuated within schools.

Even ten years ago it was rare to find serious discussion of this topic in educational circles. When Sue Pidgeon and I wrote an article on 'Gender and Reading' in *Language Matters* seven years ago, we found to our surprise that there was little literature in this area. The literature about reading in the field of gender studies tended to be critiques of bias in books and discussions of stereotyping. A prime function of literature was seen as socialisation. There was discussion of how books needed to be changed in order to eliminate overt bias and promote non-sexist attitudes. But in all this talk about texts, there was little said about children and how they were actually reading the books in question. Nor was anything said about the roles of parents and teachers, as men and women, and their influences on children's views of reading. The literature in this field tended to be written from a feminist perspective, and to focus on the presentation of women and girls in children's books, rather than on general issues of gender and reading.

In literature on reading, there was almost no acknowledgement of gender difference, except in relation to book choice. Books about initial literacy did not consider differences between girls and boys in their approaches to reading, though in one or two books, such as Margaret Clark's *Young Fluent Readers*, there was a hint of such differences – for instance, in relation to children's preferred texts for learning to read. In Clark's study of self-taught readers, boys seemed to be focusing on print in the environment in their early learning, while girls seemed to be drawn to independent reading by the desire to experience familiar stories over and over again. Since that time, despite the amount published in this field, conventional reading research has generally not addressed gender issues. In-depth studies of children learning to read, however, have tended to document the reading of girls (*Books before Five* (White, 1991), *Cushla and her Books* (Butler, 1979), *Prelude to Literacy* (Crago, 1983), *The Braid of Literature* (Wolf and Brice Heath, 1992), *Our Daughter Learns to Read and Write* (Baghban, 1984)). There has also been a routine recognition of the fact that girls are likely to do better than boys in reading assessments. But there has been no attempt to account for these differences in achievement or to relate them to the context of the assessment, the nature of the assessment, or to children's prior experience.

Among the paradoxes that characterise this area, then, is the fact that despite some of the apparent obstacles that they face in primary classrooms – the propensity of boys to seek more of the teacher's attention, and be given it; the continuing tendency of children's books to deal in stereotypes, and to show boys as more active and lively agents of their own destiny, the fact that boys have access to more powerful role models, and that men teachers tend to carry more weight and occupy more responsibility posts within the school than women teachers do – girls continue to achieve more highly than boys in reading, and to be more drawn to reading as an activity. A very few researchers, most of them women working in their own time on small-scale projects, have over the past few years been persistently asking why this should be. In the process, the focus of their interest has tended to shift. They are now more inclined to focus on issues of boys' underachievement, and on what this reveals about the links between homes and schools, the culture of primary classrooms and of boys within those classrooms, the relationships between boys and their fathers, and girls and their mothers, relationships within the peer group, and the nature of the reading curriculum. At the same time, perhaps more slowly, there has grown a realisation that girls' generally higher levels of achievement in reading may reflect the nature of the reading demands made of them, and may in fact mask substantial under-achievement in some areas of reading which, for a complex of reasons, are less carefully monitored in schools, such as the reading of information texts.

But it has not always been easy to suggest that discussions of reading and gender in the primary school needed to look beyond the existing curriculum, and beyond the usual preoccupations of work in equal

opportunities. Work on gender was mainly focused on girls and done by women. Primary school teachers, if they were interested in gender issues, were inclined to be interested in them as feminists. Discussions of gender in INSET courses tended to focus on changing the books and developing non-sexist resources. Women teachers were concerned to make more space for girls in their classrooms, and to provide them with better fictional role models.

In 1986, a media course at CLPE was thrown into disarray when the teachers were invited to view two episodes of He-Man, in order to study them as an example of a popular media fiction watched by many boys (and girls). This was at the height of the He-Man craze. Several of the teachers present, all women, were angry at being asked to take seriously something that they regarded as sexist trash. (They had never seen any of the programmes). Some walked out. They said that they would never tolerate children bringing He-Man figures into their classrooms and they wanted the course to discuss how to counteract such bad influences, rather than presenting them as legitimate material for study. Other media and gender-related courses met with similar responses.

These teachers were reacting against the He-Man phenomenon (the dolls with their gross muscles were macho stereotypes, the stories were structured around endless battles). They felt personally affronted by the kind of media initiative represented by He-Man. Heavy marketing by toy manufacturers was taking place at the level of the infant school. He-Man was followed by a whole series of highly gender-stereotyped media fictions, including My Little Pony, She-Ra, Jem, Transformers and Teenage Mutant Hero Turtles. Toymakers were using television fictions to sell these toys, and their marketing was strongly gender differentiated. These sex-stereotyped toys and fictions appeared to be popular with children, who often responded strongly to series of this kind, frequently despite parental and/or school disapproval. Several of these series had spin-off comics or books linked to them, and whether or not to buy these books for school became a serious dilemma for many teachers. They might appeal to some boys or girls, perhaps particularly to those who were not inclined to read, but for the school to buy them seemed to imply that it was condoning the sexist nature of such fictions.

This issue of the content of popular fiction remains a persistent problem for teachers. In one sense it is an aspect of the general problem of how far popular culture, street culture, can be included and studied in school. Television programmes, for instance, which are viewed by vast audiences and regularly seen by the majority of children, are often regarded as unacceptable material for school viewing. But in the He-Man story there is another element present, which has to do with the female teachers' hostility to the exaggeratedly male nature of these fictions. Such fictions are felt to be out of place in the culture of the primary school.

The world of primary education is, by and large, a female world. The majority of primary teachers are women, and the culture of a primary classroom might be described as a female culture. Certainly many of the features that characterise primary classrooms – with their play corners, their emphasis on display, and their general emphasis on the creation of a home-like atmosphere – seem to reflect this culture, which is concerned with the nurturing of young children – 'infants'. When schools make links with homes in order to discuss children's progress, and support their reading, these links are generally established and carried on between women: women teachers and children's mothers.

The children's books available in the reading corner are part of this picture. They are the products of a publishing industry in which children's books are viewed as having less status than books for adults. In children's publishing, most of the work is done by women. Women are the children's book editors, the children's book reviewers, and the children's librarians. To be widely published, promoted, bought for public consumption, and stocked in primary classrooms, a book for children must be recognised, appreciated, and selected by a group of predominantly middle-class (white) women. How far does the female culture of primary classrooms and of the world of children's books affect the choice of books available and children's attitudes to reading?

Pip Osmont (Osmont and Davis, 1987) found that most of the girls she interviewed in her small-scale study of gender and children's reading were satisfied with the choice of books available to them in their primary classroom reading corners. Their choices of books tended to coincide with those of their teachers, and they did not report that their reading at home was significantly different from their reading at school. The boys in her sample, however, tended to be less satisfied with the books available to them in school. They said that at home they read different kinds of material, and they specifically mentioned comics and media-related fictions, bought at newsagents rather than in children's bookshops. They would have liked some of this kind of reading to be available at school.

Behind all discussions of the books we make available in school are assumptions about the way in which literature works, and works on us. Discussions of gender stereotyping in children's fiction have sometimes tended to assume that readers are moulded by their reading, which presents them with 'models' that they relate to in a relatively direct and unproblematic sense. Readers are said to be constructed or produced by the text or texts they read; located, placed, or positioned in relation to the text. The passive forms of these verbs are significant: this view of reading and acculturation sees the reader as a passive rather than an active subject. The production of non-sexist fiction therefore becomes a question of offering alternative ways of being, other and preferable models, through presenting children with alternative realistic fictions, and/or of awakening the critical and resistant sense in readers, so that they may become more active and questioning in their reading.

Yet as Valerie Walkerdine points out, this approach "assumes a passive learner, or rather a rationalist one, who will change as a result of receiving the correct information about how things really are". Readers are not, on the whole, as helpless and passive as early work on sexism and literature made them appear: nor are they neutrally rational. Reading of any kind is an active and personal process in which readers have at least to willingly cooperate: "the text has to be actively read in order to engage with the way in which images and other signs, verbal and non-verbal, are constructed". (Walkerdine, 1990)

One of the major advances of very recent years in the field of gender in education has been the effort made to reconcile early ideas about 'learning gender' with what is known about children's learning in gen-eral. It is important that working theories of reading should be of a piece with theories of learning, and not detached from them: a broad cognitivist view of children as active meaning-makers, engaged in hypothesising about the world and testing their hypotheses, needs to inform our understanding of how they read as well as how they learn. Rosenblatt's view of the reader as an active participant in the reading process, bringing past experience and present personality to the text, is a very necessary corrective to those approaches that have presented the text as acting upon and constructing a passive and unresisting reader.

Charles Sarland's (1991) study of teenagers' reading, for instance, shows girls and boys reacting very differently to books, and putting their own readings on the same texts. Sarland's book deals with the sub-culture of popular fiction of the kind that teenagers read out of school, and provides interesting insights into the way young people read these kinds of texts. In some of the groups he studied, both girls and boys had read the same horror and action novels, for instance, but taken different things from them. The boys' reading of one novel (*First Blood*, the book of the first Rambo film) "concentrates on male power and integrity, which are exemplified in the action". They "were irritated by the psychologising of the book, feeling that it interrupted the action". The girls, on the other hand, were "much more responsive to details that render the characters human...recognising that they have feelings and past histories that affect their behaviour in the present". Sarland points out that it is not that the girls do not read for the action, "it is rather that they also read for the relationships and the characterisation".

Moreover the girls in the study did not reject texts of this kind because they were 'boys' books'. Instead, they found "things in the book that enable them to read it differently from the boys...(they) do not so much read different parts of the text from the boys, as read the same parts with quite contrary effects". Sarland suggests that they sometimes engaged in reading quite deliberately against the macho values of such texts. The boys, on the other hand, would not even contemplate reading books that dealt with female experience. They were adamant in their rejection of any book that seemed to them in any way like a 'girls' book', because of its content, its title, or the picture on its cover. These kinds of responses will be very familiar to teachers of younger boys, who often hear complaints of "that's a girls' book, miss".

As Sarland implies, and as Sue Adler will point out later in this book, this difference between boys and girls in their readiness to engage with fiction that deals with female and male experience means that girls get access to a wider range of fictions and of human and literary experience. They are able to sample and appraise boys' preferred fictions, and what these reveal of male culture and values, and to enjoy some aspects of them, as well as pursuing their own preferred fictional interests. Boys, on the other hand, resist the mere thought of engaging with female experience in fiction, and thus narrow the range of their literary and virtual experiences to what they can immediately identify with.

Jane Miller, in *Women Writing about Men*, suggests that all women are bilingual as readers and writers, and points out the advantages of such bilingualism, as well as the fact that it may involve "splits and instabilities, impersonation, a stepping out of yourself". The kind of impersonation described here begins early: James Britton (1982) gives us one striking example of it:

> A girl of eight was asked what sort of things she like reading. "Well," she said, "there's *Treasure Island* – that's a bloody one for when I'm feeling boyish. And there's *Little Men* – a sort of half way one." "Don't you ever feel girlish?" she was asked. "Yes, when I'm tired. Then I read *The Smallest Dormouse*."

If, in Charlotte Bronte's words "women·read men more truly than men read women", it must, in part at least, derive from this learned bilingualism or androgyny, this ability to engage with male experience in fictional form and arrive at one's own reading of it.

There were differences in Sarland's study not only between the boys' and girls' interpretations of the texts, but also between the ways that they discussed their reading. The girls'·talk about fiction flowed between talk about the text, and talk about their lives. In James Britton's terms, it was all talk in the 'spectator role', in which there were clear continuities between the girls' responses to the fictional experiences of the characters in the book, and their discussion of their own experiences and those of their friends. D.W.Harding, in *Psychological Processes in the Reading of Fiction*, draws a parallel between the reader of a novel, and a person engaging in ordinary gossip. This is how the girls seemed to be taking on their reading: they were constantly reviewing and reflecting on their experience and making links between fiction and life.

The boys, on the other hand, provided no examples of this kind of talk. "Nowhere on the tapes do boys produce these sorts of discussion about behaviour, either between the sexes or in singe-sex peer groups. It is, of course, what tends to get dismissed by paternalistic culture as 'gossip'". Sarland describes the boys as finding themselves in the text – he sees them as projecting themselves into the stereotyped characters of their preferred fictions – and the girls as 'finding the texts in themselves', though he observes that it is probable that both processes are two sides of the same coin.

It does seem that literature can work on us, and that we can use literature, in these two ways. We can seek to confirm who we are through our reading, and to find ourselves reflected in the book – and in this case we choose texts that we know are likely to legitimise our experience and support our view of ourselves, and avoid those which we feel may challenge that view. Or we can seek to extend who we are, and through the opportunity to participate in other lives and consciousnesses that literature offers us, we can take into ourselves experiences that may be very different from our own. We can find ourselves in a book, or we can find the book in ourselves, by linking it to aspects of ourselves and of our lives, and making connections with other ways of being. Margaret Meek Spencer's view, that children, in particular, read fiction in order to construct 'virtual futures' for themselves, suggests that this potential in fiction for either confirming or challenging the reader's experience may be important in shaping not only the present but the future idea of self.

Celia Burgess Macey's 1992 study of girls' writing in the primary school finds that boys' and girls' writing differs in very similar ways to their reading. The stories of the girls in the groups she worked with often featured domestic or family themes, and included "a lot of interpersonal exchanges and conversations that focus attention on the relationships between characters. Feelings are often explicitly referred to in descriptions". None of the girls had written stories in which they themselves were the main characters, and they generally wrote in the third person. By contrast, the boys' stories were much more action-packed.

Feelings were much less apparent and there was less use of dialogue, except where it was needed to move the action along. Very often the boys wrote in the first person or wrote stories about themselves. They appeared in their own stories in heroic roles, sometimes associated with media heroes.

The girls that Burgess Macey interviewed were very conscious of the differences between boys' and girls' writing. Both boys and girls tended to write for their own sex, and boys were disinclined to read girls' stories. One girl said:

> I write my stories for girls to read really. Boys mostly read their own sto-ries. They write about guns and things. *The Secret Hiding Place* sounds like an adventure story but when they think it's been written by a girl they just think it's not very good and they don't bother to read inside. Well, I haven't seen any boys reading it.

Any discussion of girls and boys as readers cannot be confined only to academic questions of literary response. Development as a reader is clearly linked to development as a person, and to emotional attitudes. Both the boys in Sarland's research and those in Burgess Macy's study seemed to reject quite flatly the opportunities that reading and writing present for exploring inner worlds of feeling, perhaps because they saw this kind of exploration as incompatible with their view of themselves as males. The OFSTED report (1993) found "little evidence of boys discussing the affective aspects of experience or of their writing with conviction about personal feelings". Certainly the girls interviewed by Burgess Macy saw boys as very different from themselves in their behaviour and particularly in their attitudes to feelings, in a way that was clearly linked to their view of the differences between girls' and boys' writing:

> Boys don't talk to their friends about being upset. They just isolate each other and say "go away and sort it out yourself". I think grown-up women have more friends than men do. They go and see their friends more – like my mum goes and sees her friends, and she can chat to them and tell them all her personal stuff that she can't discuss with her hus-band.

The gossip that is literature may have stronger continuities with other aspects of their lives for girls than it does for boys.

I have been talking about the reading of fiction almost exclusively in this introduction, and very often in primary schools 'reading' and 'reading fiction' are used virtually synonymously. By and large we provide children with fictional material as the staple ingredient of early reading pro-grammes, and judge their developing ability as readers by their ability to read more extended fictions, and to respond to fiction. But any considera-tion of reading and gender must also take into account the reading of information texts, and how boys and girls approach this kind of material.

The surveys show that boys are far more interested in reading information books than girls are. Though they are less likely than girls to choose to explore the inner world of feeling that literature gives access to, they are far more likely to choose to explore the external world of facts through their reading. They may be more comfortable, also, with the impersonal style of information writing, and with factual genres. It has been clear for a long time now that this kind of reading is given less attention in primary schools, is less carefully recorded and supported, and that less thought is generally given to what constitutes progress and development in non-fiction reading. Our views of girls' and boys' relative strengths as readers might be altered in the context of a reading curriculum which took more carefully into account boys' reading interests, and set out to develop them.

Girls are less inclined to choose to read information texts, and this disinclination may reflect both an unwillingness to engage with the 'other world' that print gives access to – the world outside the self, the outer world of action and physical reality – and a feeling that this kind of way of engaging with the world is somehow incompatible with their sense of themselves as females. Conventional views of what constitutes scientific or factual writing may help to perpetuate this state of affairs, and many writers have argued for the importance of recognising narrative as a legitimate way of writing in science (Fox, 1990; Strube, 1990).

Girls' less extensive experience of recreational reading in this area may mean that their ability to engage with certain kinds of learning is less developed; they may lack the spontaneous concepts which are often taken for granted in some curriculum areas, and on which later academic learning will build. And unless their reading of texts other than fictional texts is given more deliberate support, and their appreciation of other genres more positively encouraged, they may find themselves handicapped when they come to use their reading in their learning across the curriculum.

In all this, teachers are not neutral. We ourselves are women, or men, and we are readers and writers with our own preferences, which we are likely to communicate to our pupils. We may also, unconsciously, collude with them, perhaps by tacitly conveying the view that some kinds of reading are much less important than others. It is clear that children's views of males and females as readers are very strongly influenced by their experience of adult readers, initially their experience of their parents, and thereafter of the other adults whom they come into contact with. In this book, we examine the role of parents and peer groups in shaping children's views of gender and reading. But we also consider how teachers can make a difference to such views, and visit some class-rooms where they are doing so. The first of the main findings of the OFSTED report on *Boys and English* states that "The crucial factor in boys' attitudes towards English and their performance in the subject was the influence of the teacher". The report also points out that in class-rooms where boys were achieving better, expectations of all pupils were high, and both girls and boys benefited from this.

In Vygotsky's term, reading is a psychological tool, a tool which is used to operate on the world – both in the ordinary sense of using func-tional literacy to find our way about the world, and in a more complex sense, by giving readers potential access to infinities of alternative worlds, any of which may affect the way we view the immediate world, subtly change it for us, or enable us to operate differently within it. We hope that the different articles in this book, by opening up ways of viewing the topic of gender and reading, will suggest possibilities, opportunities, and alternatives. A distinguishing feature of psychological tools is that they also turn back on their users; they have a transforming quality. Like all such tools reading can be used reflexively, in order to change ourselves. That is why discussions of gender and reading can never be too gloomily deterministic – all readers, wherever they begin, may arrive at unexpected destinations.

MYRA BARRS

A Reading History

VALERIE WALKERDINE

Actually, the first memory about my reading history that comes to mind is not about reading at all, but a knowledge of words. I was on a coach trip with my parents and younger sister. I must have been about six and as the coach came to the top of a hill with a rather wide and spectacular view of Derbyshire, I remarked "Oh, what a wonderful panorama". My startled parents practically told the whole bus that I had used this long and rather exotic word, panorama. I learnt, of course, what an impression words could have. I learnt too, that such erudition was thought to be precocious and very clever. I have no doubt that the bus occupants were impressed. I think I learnt the word at school and maybe from my reading, but actually I remember little about my early reading history except that I learnt to read at school using those Janet and John and cat-sat-on-the-mat type reading books and that Julia Goddard's mother complained to mine that I was being used to teach her daughter to read.

I'm sure my parents read stories to me, but I can't remember any. What I do remember though, is that I loved the flower fairies books that were popular in the 1950s and still available today. I think there was an alphabet with a flower fairy and poem for each letter. How I dreamed of being like those fairies, tiny, beautiful little creatures, so diminutive and yet so powerful. It was perhaps a way of imagining being small and loved and yet having one's wishes fulfilled, indeed to make dreams come true. I have written at length elsewhere about how those little fairies fitted well both with the image of me as a bluebell fairy winning the local fancy dress competition at three and the nickname that my father had for me, Tinky, short for Tinkerbell.

I loved those books because of all the powerful fantasies that caught me inside them, like a spider in a web and which I caught and held to make sense of myself, of being a girl, of growing up. I liked too the book of Grimm's fairy tales that had belonged to my mother as a child, in which there were wonderful illustrations, beautiful plates with line drawings and vibrant colours. Perhaps it was because drawing meant more than anything else to me as a child that it is the illustrations of the books that I remember best. I don't remember myself as a great early childhood reader; I was certainly not the sort of child who always had her nose in a book.

We didn't have many books at home, but this should not be mistaken as a lack of interest in reading on my family's part. Books were very expensive before the advent of paperbacks (which did not emerge until Penguin started them when I was at grammar school: then and only then was I encouraged by the school to actually *buy* books). My mother in particular was an avid reader who borrowed books from the local library every week. I remember it very well. Often I would walk with her to the wooden village hall which housed the library several days per week. On these days the librarians arrived to open up the display cases of books and we used to wander around, browsing. She read mostly romantic fiction and historical novels. I gradually went through the children's classics and graduated onto - well, the ones I most remember - were in a series about 'the Whiteoaks of Jalna' by Mazo de la Roche! I liked the browsing, the tickets, the taking of the pile of books and returning them for others.

We never really entered bookshops but that certainly did not mean that we never read. I feel angry often when I hear once again the usual diatribes about working class parents who don't care about reading and their children's education. It is the level of ignorance about working class reading practices which particularly annoys me, along with the moralising. Yes, I read books about flower fairies, comics, encyclopaedias and later 'Woman', 'Woman's Own', the 'People', the 'News of the World' and the 'Derby Evening Telegraph' and of course, since they were part of my world, I liked them very much. Reading them did not stop me becoming an academic, indeed one who has written her fair share of books. So, the complexities of subjectivity and how we become what we are lost on those who insist that socialisation is the work of agents, especially parents, who may be blamed for having rendered their children sexist for life by allowing them to read girly stories or trashy comics.

Perhaps that is why I am prepared now in my own work to look at what forms of popular media and literature mean to those that read them, and am not prepared to simply toss them away as so much useless garbage. Sure, now I read the 'Guardian' and not the 'Sun', but that does not mean that I don't also get voyeuristic pleasure from reading about the latest Royal exploits or the lives of film stars. Or that I am willing to call moronic the readers of such material just because others are not prepared to attempt to understand the complexity of the lives in which such reading has a place. What I mean, is that flower fairies, The Whiteoaks of Jalna, encyclopaedias, all caught me up inside a world of my imagination. The fantasy space created using the materials available to me was important in forming my creativity. Those who insist in a cognitivist way that mothers or fathers pass on habits and that those habits may be towards trash and therefore not about 'real learning' or the 'best literature' are missing the point about the world both created for me and which I created with the tools available to me.

Back to my childhood. My father bought a set of encyclopaedias called *The Book of Knowledge* from a door-to-door salesman. I really liked these and often made up my own little books, copying out information and pictures from them. For example, I still have one little book I made, called 'Children and costumes of other lands', which was heavily into the exotic. Perhaps that early experience of creative authorship gave me valuable lessons in the sense that I did not only read books, I made them for myself, but then I always had little projects on the go, long before project work became common in primary schools. What is clear is that reading for me was never a passive activity, it if ever is for any reader. I imagined, I dreamed, I created, just as I am still doing to this day. One of the central points in my life as an academic and a writer was formed then. The capacity to dream and to create, using reading as a tool, were learnt in those early days.

But it was at grammar school that I had to hang on hard to that creativity in the face of derision from teachers and other pupils about the newspapers we took, or the girls who roundly castigated me because I thought that the story that I liked in the 'Girl' comic, 'Belle of the ballet', was pronounced 'belly' to rhyme with ballet (bally in Derbyshire). I missed Belly of the Ballet when I had to learn that this was not correct, just as I missed the tabloids when it was suggested that I try the (incomprehensible) 'Daily Telegraph', which I paid for with money from my paper round. What I remember then of my peers is simply the happy acceptability of my creativity at primary school and a middle class culture that nearly stifled it at grammar school. Perhaps that is why I feel so angry about all those remarks about inculcation of the 'wrong' habits.

Those early practices that created and sustained me as a reader and writer do so to this day. I still find fertile ground in the richness of my fantasies, fantasies created with fairies who looked like flowers, damsels with beautifully painted costumes and tales of worlds about which I could then only dream. I am not saying that at the very least there aren't contradictions in those very fantasies but I do want to acknowledge their sustaining power in the formation of the adult that I am today.

VALERIE WALKERDINE

CHILDREN

AND

PARENTS

Learning Reading and Learning Gender

SUE PIDGEON

I am teaching in the reception class, and we are starting the day with 'news'. Dean tells us about his weekend visit to his grandparents' caravan, Carol talks about a birthday party, and Dipak shows us his new trainers. "They're boys' shoes, Miss" he adds. I'm surprised. Both boys and girls wear trainers. "How can you tell?" I say. He seems a little perplexed, but then he and some of the other boys look at them closely; "Because of this" he says, and they point out to me the logo, the picture of the Turtles. I am surprised because, throughout the term, I have thought that we have been actively trying to promote equality, and I am puzzled that even shoes should be viewed as needing to be gender-specific.

Later in the day I look at the group settling down for 'quiet reading'. The girls are quietly, and generally individually, choosing from the known texts; they are choosing sensibly and carefully, as I would expect, since we have worked hard to establish this quiet reading time. They are choosing the favourite song book, fairy stories, and other well-known texts. Pretty soon they are mainly settled. Why is it then that the boys seem to be trying to choose in groups? One group is fighting over the *Zoo Guide*, another over a shared-reading version of *Bear Hunt*. Once again the question of gender rises within me. I wonder, can it be that children who are prepared to think about shoes in terms of 'boys' shoes' or 'girls' shoes' are thinking similarly about books and reading?

Are *Titch, Rosie's Walk, Bear Hunt*, boys' books or girls' books? I don't know, I used not to consider it. It never seemed to be of much concern to the children I've shared them with. In fact they seem to have been enjoyed with equal gusto by boys and girls alike. But are children perhaps reading different things into these experiences with books? We know that by the age of seven, marked differences between girls' and boys' reading abilities and reading preferences can be identified. These differences are perpetuated and become more obvious throughout school and into adulthood. How do these differences emerge, and why? Can it be that, right from the beginning of children's reading experiences, they are linking these experiences with what they know about gender? When I first became interested in this topic I thought that there might be a simple way of affecting the situation, like changing the books themselves. This was at a time when equal opportunities policies tended to focus on issues of bookstock. Now I am reconciled to the fact that there are no simple answers where gender is concerned.

When thinking around the topic of gender and reading, I became increasingly interested in the question of how children learn about gender in the first place, and whether this has any relevance to how they perceive reading. From observing my own children and those I taught, I had noticed that at particular moments in development, gender-specific behaviour had seemed to become important to them. Certainly around five seemed to be one of these moments. I remember when my daughter at about this age suddenly refused to wear trousers to school. (Yet when she was about twelve she would *only* wear trousers to school). My son, like those of my friends, was at a certain point suddenly determined that he had to have a 'gun' to play with, and despite my steady resistance, proceeded to use any object as a 'gun'. I connected incidents like these preoccupations with stereotypical behaviour with ways of marking gender in my reception class. I wondered if it was significant that the children's apparent spurt of interest in gender-related behaviour seemed to occur at around the same time that they were 'learning to read'.

Before children officially begin to learn to read they are already 'reading' the world around them, and bringing to this process all the skills of taking meaning from context that they will later draw on in their reading of text. Among the key pieces of learning they focus on is learning about gender. We may assume that this is because they appreciate from early on the fundamental importance of this concept to everybody they know. So before ever children begin to decode print, they have begun to decode gender. But I wanted to consider whether these two kinds of learning might interrelate in any way. Both topics have been the subject of much writing, much research, and much disagreement, but interest has rarely focused the relationship between the two. I felt that in order to understand this relationship I needed more information on how children learn about gender, and how this is linked to other aspects of their learning. I also wanted to talk to some children and get their perspective on gender and reading. Did they think that men and women were different as readers, and that they read different things? And did they think this was important ?

CHILDREN'S DEVELOPING UNDERSTANDING
OF GENDER DIFFERENCE

Gender difference affects every aspect of how we live, and how we are perceived. Historically, it is a difference that is built into the power structures of society, and it is really only during this century that these divisions have been questioned and challenged. Gender differences begin to be learnt from birth, and deeply affect our identity. For each one of us, our experiences as a girl or a boy, woman or man, are an integral part of our own life story.

The tremendous interest in these differences mean that they have been studied and argued over by biologists, sociologists, and psychologists, as well as by people in general. The fact that there is considerable disagreement over both the reasons for gender differences and how individuals come to be 'located' in relation to them, makes it clear that we do not really know how gender is learnt. Sociology and biology have developed theories about the sexual divisions in society, and psychologists have been concerned with the reasons for this. "...Psychology accepts the reality of gender and its components, particularly gender identity and gender role. The 'fact' of masculinity and femininity (adherence to a particular gender role) is as real and objective for psychology as hormones are for biology" (Kessler and McKenna, 1978). But is gender identity born in you, really part of your hormones, or is it learnt as part of the general learning of life, gradually, over time, and from experiences?

Because children are born one sex or the other does not mean that they are born with the appropriate gender attributes or behaviour. How do boys and girls know how to behave in appropriate ways? Differing psychological approaches have suggested differing theories; the biological determinist's theory differs from the social learning theory, the cognitive-developmental theory, and the psychoanalytic theory. As Janet Sayers suggests in *Psychology and Gender Divisions,* each of these theories makes important points but cannot totally explain how individuals 'acquire' gender. Nor can any psychological theory can explain why gender is such an important social division, and how children become aware of the importance of these divisions. But what do psychological theories tell us about how children learn about gender? We need to briefly review these.

Biological determinists have tried to argue that biological differences account for psychological differences, and that it is hormones that make men more competitive and women more nurturing. Writers such as de Lacoste-Uamsing and Holloway (1982) suggest that boys are better at visual and spatial tasks because their brains are better adapted to such tasks. Neurologist Richard M. Restak argues that there are differences in function between men's and women's brains that account for gender differences. Although studies like these cannot be dismissed, their findings are far from conclusive. They generally run up against the chicken-and-the-egg problem. We cannot assume that biological differences account for gender differences, because of the obvious link between gender and social roles.

Social learning is seen by many researchers as being the key determinant of gender-related behaviour. It seems fairly obvious that some aspects of gender are learnt as children are treated as either boys or girls, and begin to decode what this means. There is plenty of evidence to show that children *are* treated differently from birth, depending on whether they are a boy or a girl. There are differences in how they are handled, physically and emotionally (Pitcher and Schultz, 1983), how behavior is interpreted (Walum, 1977), and how they are spoken to (Hassan, 1984). Girls and boys are given different toys to play with and come to choose different kinds of play, (boys tending to prefer cars, construction activities, and more physical play, with girls opting for more sedentary and domestic play). In all these areas, children's personal experiences, the expectations of adults, and images from the media will all affect their development.

But social learning is not enough in itself to explain how children learn about gender difference. Social learning is limited by the idea of cause and effect, but in fact our social experiences do not necessarily determine our behaviour. Gender is not learnt only by imitation; the learner needs to play an active part in the process. In other words, the learner has some 'choice' over what they learn. Children who suddenly assert their own views of what is gender-appropriate are evidence that they have not learnt only by imitating those in their immediate surroundings.

Learning gender, then, is also related to children's cognitive development, and cognitive psychologists suggest that children will be building up a concept of gender, or rather a series of concepts, through their experiences, and in accordance with their stage of intellectual development. Learning about gender, in this way of viewing things, will follow the same developmental pattern as other concepts, from concrete to abstract. The Piagetian developmental psychologist Lawrence Kohlberg has looked at children's intellectual understanding of gender. He maintains that only when children are able to identify themselves correctly as a boy or as a girl does gender become important to them. He notes that that they can usually do this by the age of three. Subsequently, broadly between the ages of three and seven, children become aware of the concept of gender difference, and it becomes a key issue for them.

Although most three year olds can correctly identify their own sex and that of others, they are only at the beginning of their understanding of this complex concept and may not realise, for instance, that sex is a permanent attribute. An understanding of the permanence of gender is important, because only when children are sure that, whatever they do, they will still remain a boy or a girl, can they progress beyond very crude versions of what behaviour is gender-appropriate.

Cognitively, children develop their concept of gender through building hypotheses based on their experience. As in the development of other concepts at this age, initially they pay most attention to externals – physical attributes, behaviour – and conclude that these are of overriding importance. Gender is a complex concept, and it is hardly surprising that initially children pick up on the most obvious and often most stereotypical differences. This helps to explain why, at around five, gender-appropriate behaviour is particularly important to children, and why young children at this stage move towards stereotypical behaviours (sometimes to the consternation of their more liberal parents and teachers). They are often anxious to identify attributes as male or female, and may insist on behaviour appropriate to their gender, and vehemently condemn or reject those they associate with the 'wrong' gender. But once the concept of permanent gender identity is established (around age ten) they no longer see sex-role differences as absolute, but as more of social convention that can be changed.

Certainly cognitive development theory does shed light on the process of how children learn gender identity, but it also cannot stand alone. It helps us to understand why children should put such an emphasis on outward and visible differences when defining gender. But it does not explain how children become aware of the deeper significance of gender and how they understand that gender differences are of fundamental importance to all those around them.

The perspective that has not been touched on yet is the one that considers gender and sexuality. Classic psychoanalytic theory stressed the importance of children's awareness of sexuality at around age four. Although Freud's interpretations have been questioned, and many alternatives to his initial theory have been proposed, it is still necessary when looking at children's understanding to include some perspective that goes deeper than cognitive thought and acknowledges the role of the unconscious, the affective, and the emotional in all that relates to children's learning about gender. The post-Freudian Nancy Chuderov emphasises the differences in the mother/child relationship as the key to sex differences, and suggests that mothers relate to sons as being 'different', while they 'merge' more with their daughters. As a result, children grow up with differing capacities for relationships, boys with a definite sense of separateness, girls with a sense of empathy.

These psychological theories help to elucidate how children learn about gender. Interestingly, they suggest that the years around five are particularly important, and this may be relevant when we bear in mind that this is the time when children are going to school and learning to read. But none of these theories is adequate by itself to explain the process of learning gender. And what these theories omit is the wider view of what it actually means within a culture or society to be a boy or girl .

TALKING TO CHILDREN

It seemed necessary to talk to some children to get find out what learning gender means to them. I spoke to a random group between the ages of four and nine. I was particularly interested in the six year olds, because I thought that by six, children would be beginning to establish views of themselves both as readers and as boys or girls.

It is often difficult to draw out accurately the implications of what children are saying, but I think it is possible, from what these children say, to throw some light upon their understanding of gender difference. You can see this from the conversation that I had with Nadia and Claudia .

Sue:	What are the differences between boys and girls, do you think?
Nadia:	(*spells out the letters*) P-A-N-T-S.
Claudia:	Boys play football. Girls like going to discos and things like that.
Sue:	Do you mean trousers 'pants' or knickers 'pants'?
Nadia:	Knickers pants. They wear boxer shorts and trousers.
Claudia:	And if it's a really cool day, they wear T-shirts. They like to play chasing or playing tennis or playing catch.

The two girls are focusing on dress and behaviour, the outward visual characteristics that make boys different from them. The responses of four chidren from ages four to nine to the same question suggest how their understanding of gender is developing.

Anya, age four, knows that she is a girl and that when she grows up she will also 'be a girl'. When we talked about how we knew if someone was a boy or girl she said

Anya:	Because I do...because I can see they are...because I can see they got long hair. I can see they got a bathing suit. (*We were on holiday at the time.*)

Anya is drawing on her immediate experience and her immediate surroundings to define boys and girls by appearance.

Clara, age seven, is doing the same thing, but trying to generalise a bit more.

Clara:	Girls wear skirts, dresses, and have long hair, most girls. And boys wear trousers most of the time, and have short hair.
Sue:	At school do boys and girls do different things?
Clara:	Yes. Mostly girls like to do drawing and painting. Boys

like writing long stories, because most of the boys do write long stories. In the playground boys are most interested in playing football. Girls like playing hopscotch, skipping rope games, and hoops.

Apparently, there are some very good writers in her class who are boys, and she has absorbed this into her general classification of boys' behaviour. As in all concept formation, this presumably will remain part of her concept of gender difference until challenged by some experience that does not fit neatly into her framework. It's interesting that she focuses on games with rules in her attempt to elucidate the rules of gender-specific behaviour.

But David, age seven, is really having problems sorting out what girls are 'meant' to look like, and how it conflicts with his actual experience. Talking about how you can tell if someone is a boy or a girl, he says

David: You can tell...really you can tell...I don't know how...You would know... you wouldn't know because some girls like Mum and Guilia (his sister) don't have a dress.

By nine, his brother Daniel is able to move quite beyond his actual personal experience and make relative generalisations. He says

Daniel: Usually girls have long hair and usually wear skirts, while boys usually wear jeans and wear very short hair.

The 'usually' is important. Daniel can see that many of the ways of identifying boys or girls are conventions. He should be able, theoretically anyway, to discuss exceptions to his generalisations; his concept of gender has the capacity to change and expand.

The younger children are not yet at this point. They are still at the stage when what things look like, their physical properties, override anything else they know. But looking at these examples helps to clarify the complexity of the idea of gender and how children try to make it make sense to themselves.

Cognitive psychologists argue that once children develop stable gender identites and know that they are a boy or a girl, they begin to prefer gender-typed activites and objects. This is because children value, and wish to be like, those they perceive as similar to themselves. As Kohlberg states it, their thinking is: "I am a boy. Therefore I like boy things. Therefore doing boy things is rewarding" (Kessler and McKenna, 1978). Children's behaviour changes at this stage, and they tend to move into single-sex friendship groups, and to consider activities (and clothes) as belonging to 'boys' or 'girls'. The peer group begins to be a key influence on their sense of themselves.

You can see this when the boys talk about the differences between boys and girls with me.

Sue: What do boys like doing?
Harry: They like to play
Alex: I've got a water pistol. They like having a water pistol so they can say 'hands up' and squirt water...
Sue: What about the girls?
Alex: They like playing with dollies.
Harry: They like playing with dollies.

The two boys' generalisations are based on what they have noticed (girls and dollies) and their own experiences (boys and water pistols). But we can assume that there are multiple influences on how they make sense of this experience. These influences are going to come from adults and siblings, from their own lives, from the media, and from all the many ways in which experience is represented in their society. Implicit within this simple conversation, in fact, are wider issues to do power and social roles – is it chance that guns and dolls are what they pick on in order to illustrate difference?

It is in play, and especially in imaginative play, that children are able to play out and explore experiences they are grappling with, and particularly to begin to try to make sense of adult roles. Vivian Paley in her great book *Boys and Girls, Superheroes in the Doll Corner* charts the gender differences in children's play in her Chicago kindergarten, and concludes that, although their play seemed steroetypical, it also seemed to be a part of their developing understanding of gender roles.

> The four year old boy is less comfortable in the doll corner than he was the year before...the superhero clique has formed and the doll corner is becoming the women's room...The atmosphere in the doll corner changes dramatically among five-and six-year olds. The doll corner in fact is entering its final phase in which girls and boys try to end lingering confusion about the roles they play, roles they will now examine in a predominantly social context...Both seek a new 'social' definition for 'boy' and 'girl'. They search everywhere for clues, hoping to create separate and final images.'

Imaginative play allows young children to play out gender roles, but play gradually changes and becomes more rule governed. Picher and Schultz note

> We notice a lot of nurturance in girls' pretend play, at ages three, four and five, but it is only at five that girls begin to apply their fantasised sex-roles in games with rules and in real situations.

I too noticed this when I watched the six year olds playing in the home corner. The appropriate gender-related (and often apparently stereotypical) behaviours were obviously agreed between the players. Saying 'Pretend I'm the Mummy' or 'the doctor' or 'Batman' was shorthand for such understood behaviours and there was considerable disagreement if one player went outside what was deemed apropriate to that role. The gender roles in play also seem to reflect the developing concept of gender. When Adam tells me that he plays 'mummies and daddies' at home he tells me is the father or the boy. When I ask if he is ever the mother he replies 'No, certainly not' and shakes his head, vehemently.

Contrast this with what Anya, age four, says about it.

> Just normally girls play in the home corner. Someone bes the baby and Hetty likes to be the mum. Raquel just fusses to be the baby and I be the big sister, or sometimes Raquel likes to be the dad. Sometimes Raquel wears leggings or dungarees. Sometimes Lloyd or Hugh like to be the dad.

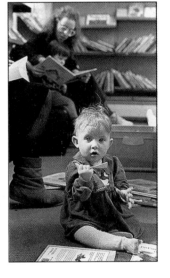

I think here we can see her beginning to grapple with ideas of gender identity. She seems to imply that its alright for Raquel to be the dad – if she's wearing trousers. However it is worth commenting that among the whole group I questioned only a girl suggested that it was acceptable for a girl to play the father, while no boy suggested that it was alright for a boy to be the mother. I noticed similar things when I was working with a year 2 class on changing fairy tales. We had had lengthy discussions about gender roles and possibilities of changing traditional stories. When they rewrote the stories, many children were happy to write 'Jill and the Beanstalk', but no one wanted to write' The Sleeping Prince'. Gender is a subject on which it is hard to be neutral.

By age nine, Daniel is able to be more analytical about gender differences in relation to games that are played. Possibly, also, he is beginning to have some implicit understanding of the power relations involved in play.

Daniel: Well, boys like adventure but don't like playing things like families. Girls like playing things like one's father and one's mother. The problem is with girls is that they all have a fight because they all want to be mother and no one wants to be father.

Sue: Do you ever play you are a girl in games?

Daniel: No. Since we're boys we always play with boys, and no boy wants to be a girl. Everyone in our class says boys against girls because they say girls are wimps.

Sue: What do the girls say about the boys?

Daniel: The problem is that the girls go along with the boys and they say 'We want some boys on our side'.

When I started talking to the children I had not expected them to be so aware of gender difference or so concerned about it. I think I somehow expected them to have 'acquired' the concept whole. Nor had I expected the very conventional divisions between boys as active and girls as domestic to be so apparent in the children, and so much part of their view of others and themselves. It is around age five that children seem to be particularly attentive to this complex concept and, as we noted, there is considerable agreement between different schools of psychology (cognitive, social, and psychanalytic) that this age is a particularly important one for learning about gender. Is it possible that children take this heightened awareness of gender with them to their learning to read? And, if so, is this simply because at this age all areas of experience are being earnestly scrutinised for their significance in relation to gender (boys' trainers and girls' trainers), or because reading itself is not a neutral activity but one that is strongly related to gender roles?

GENDER-RELATED READING BEHAVIOUR

We know that there are differences in reading choices and reading ability between men and women, boys and girls, and that these are apparent by seven. Being aware of how important gender is to these young children, I wanted to see if this awareness was part of their perceptions about reading, and if judgements about what was appropriate for boys and girls were already affecting their reading choices and reading behaviours.

Recently, writers Hilary Minns (1990) and Shirley Payton (1984) have illustrated how much children learn about reading from home, and Shirley Brice Heath (1983) has shown that children also learn how literacy is used in their communities. I wondered how far this learning related to issues of gender. It would have been useful to look at gender-related studies of children's experiences of reading at home, but as far as I know, none exist. I began my questioning by trying to see how far the children were aware of men's and women's reading choices and reading habits. The six-year-old children I asked showed considerable knowledge about what men and women read and why.

Two boys talking about what their parents read say:

Alex: My daddy reads and my mummy reads.

Harry: My mummy and my daddy are always into newspapers. Because at this moment there's this thing going on about the Channel tunnel and they're reading about that. (*There was a possibility that the Channel tunnel train route might pass through the neighbourhood at the time and a great deal of support had been amassed against it*).

Two other boys say similar things:

Sue: What do your mummy and daddy read?
Andrew: Radio Times, the newspaper and the TV Times.
Sue: Do they read books?
Andrew: They read grown-up books
Darren: My mum doesn't read the newspapers, my dad does.

The girls introduce some evaluative comments into their observations:

Kathy: Yeah, my mum reads....she reads books like romance
          books to get her to sleep that are rubbish.
Sue: Why are they rubbish?
Kathy: Because they've got all romance things in.
Naomi: My dad's got loads of medals' cos he goes shooting and
          fishing and...
Sue: Does your dad read?
Naomi: Yeah, he reads his fishing books to get all this stuff.
Sue: What about your mum, does she read?
Naomi: No, she just does all these things, she does all the washing
          up and things like that.

Many of the points that were mentioned when talking about learning gender áre apparent here. Not only have these two paid attention to reading behaviours and choices but they are also making judgements about them, presumably based on their developing understanding of gender roles in society. What they see and what they hear is building their picture of gender and reading. Two other girls describe the domestic settings that reading takes place in:

Sue: What about... do other people in your house read?
Claudia: Only my sister in the loo. She keeps getting a book and
          reading it. And then my daddy sits in a chair and reads the
          newspapers, and my mummy sits in the chair next to him
          and reads a magzine, and then in the night when Daddy is
          out I sit at the top of the stairs and I listen to Mummy and
          Jessica read magazines and saying "Do you like that girl"
          and "Look at those clothes. Why don't you buy those?"
          and the next day I see a really huge parcel and I say
          "What's in there Mum" "Well, last night I was looking in
          a magazine, and I saw some clothes!"
Sue: (laughing) Oh, I know that!
Claudia: Well they put them on and say "Aargh, I think I'll put
          them back".
Sue: Do your mum and dad read?
Nadia: Well, they're always reading the newspaper, and you know,
          them really big thick books. My mum reads them as well.
          She's got one and it's *Prime Time* Joan Collins.

I was surprised how aware and articulate these six year olds were able to be about the reasons and purposes that adults had for reading. They see that reading is for information (newspapers to find out about the Channel tunnel), functional (ordering things through magazines) and for pleasure (magazines, big thick books). But they also perceive differences related to gender. Both boys and girls describe men and women reading newspapers, but the girls focus more on the fiction read by women. Kathy adds that although romantic fiction is read for pleasure, it is also rubbish. Implicit in this is a view that women's reading preferences are less serious than men's.

Reading as an activity is closely tied up with one's perception of oneself. Margaret Clark, in her study of young fluent readers (1976) notes that reading opens two worlds to us: the public exterior world of newspapers and information, and the interior world of fiction, of empathy and feelings. She also observed that, of the children who were reading before they started school, the girls tended to have learnt to read on favourite fairy stories, while the boys had paid more attention to print in the environment. Are boys and girls, in their earliest reading attitudes, reflecting their awareness that different kinds of print are preferred by men or women, and what this, ultimately, means in terms of the different kinds of knowledge and power they give access to? The social construction of a reader seems likely to include a gender dimension. Maybe this has some bearing on how children approach reading in school.

We need to consider, also, how schools present reading to children. How far are primary classrooms, with their emphasis on stories, fiction, and quiet reading, and their predominantly female models of readers, suggesting to children that reading is more likely to be a girls' activity than a boys' activity? It is still rare for reception classes to introduce children to information reading, and many children will go through their entire infant school experience without ever seeing an adult male reader. Given children's heightened awareness of this issue, and the strong pressures on them, from within and without, to conform to type, are schools simply confirming their original stereotypical assumptions about who and what reading is for, or do they ever succeed in complicating them? I wanted to see if children saw some books as more appropriate to boys or girls. It became apparent that, although they may not be looking at every book that they come across in this way, they had already, by age seven, begun to make assumptions about the appropriateness of certain subject matter. I asked Clara, age seven, if there was a difference in the books themselves.

Clara: Yes, some books are girls' books and some books are
            boys'. There's one particular book that boys specially like,

it's very popular with the boys. It's about a cat really into music.

Sue: Oh, I know, *Curtis the HipHop Cat.*

Clara: Yeah. Girls don't really have a favourite book...girls are not really interested in dragons and things. I'm not really inter ested in those kind of things. I think its because I'm a girl.

David, age seven says similar things.

> "I like to read mystery books. Girls like books about farms probably. Boys like books about space, mystery and all things like that".

Daniel, age nine, is again able to generalize and sums it up by saying

> "Well boys like the most dangerous and scarey books while girls like calm books where nothing really happens".

These chidren find it easy to tell me the difference between boys' and girls' books. By seven, Clara and David seem to be intent on classifying 'boys' and 'girls' books into broad categories, rather as they viewed boys' and girls' clothes, appearance, or behaviour.

Similar points have been noticed when childen talk about writing. Cindy Jantsz (1993) found that when she talked to four seven year olds, they had very definite ideas about what boys and girls would like in stories. The boys thought girls would like stories about horses, and dolls, and preferred happy endings. They felt they would dislike fighting, killing, wrestling, and scary stories. The girls thought that boys enjoyed stories about boys and not girls, and that they enjoyed stories involving fighting and killing, with lots of adventure and mystery. Ghostbusters, wrestling, hero turtles, and racing were also thought to be popular, and one girl felt that if girls were present in a story then the boys in the story would want to bully them and wouldn't let them play games. This was also noted by Celia Burgess Macey in her study of girls' writing. Are chil-dren choosing certain books and writing certain stories to confirm their gender identity? And what influence does their peer group have on this urge to conform to a norm?

Reading differences go beyond the question of the choices children make, and what they read. We also need to consider how children read, and whether their experience, even their experience of the same books, is perhaps dependent on their gender. Recent work on reading has been studying reader 'response' to texts and showing that there is no one way of reading/understanding a text, but that our interpretations are affected by what we bring to it. This in turn will be affected by our life experi-ences, which will include our experiences as as a man or woman, girl or boy. Charles Sarland (1992) found, when he studied reading in sec-ondary school, that boys and girls were were focusing on very different things in the books they read, with the boys focussing more on the action, the girls on the relationships. Is this also happening with younger children? It would be interesting to follow this up and look more closely at gender and response, and at young children's 'reading' of the same texts.

Once again, in looking at gender and reading, I am left with more questions and no answers, and a feeling that there is so much still to find out. The interrelationship of gender and reading is complicated, but it would seem that reading does reflect and confirm gender identity. By the time they come to school, children are aware of what men and women around them read. How far do they use their reading to confirm their expectations of gender roles, and do their reading choices reflect their expectations of the two worlds of reading? Gender is not a neutral subject; attached to these readings, these perceptions, are all the other wider attitudes associated with gender.

It is important to remember that this does not mean that children are predestined to follow one gender-specific path in their reading development. Reading may be one of the behaviours that reflects and confirms gender identity, but it also has the potential to extend it. Concepts are built by experiences confirming or rejecting an original hypothesis. Even though young children at initial stages may need to focus on noticeable universal differences, and on sterotypical behaviours, these are constantly going to be modified by their experiences. If children are encouraged to consider alternative possibilities, if teachers and parents demonstrate these alternatives, and make apparent to the children that men and women can read all kinds of material, if the possibilities of choices beyond the stereotypical are made explicit, if discussions can open up the variety of ways in which different readers respond to texts, then both girls and boys may come to see that there are many ways of being a reader.

SUE PIDGEON

From Birth to Sixteen Months

NAIMA BROWNE

The majority of children starting school know a great deal about reading, despite not having been formally taught to read. This chapter explores a small girl's growing understanding of reading from birth to 16 months, and illustrates how her understanding of reading began to develop before she was able to talk, and long before she started formal schooling.

BIRTH TO SIX MONTHS

From the time that Rehana was born, she had been given a range of picture books. At around the age of four months she began to show a particular interest in the pictures in books; her eyes would focus on the picture and scan it. At this stage, bright, complex pictures were a favourite. She looked at pictures in books and magazines whilst sitting on an adult's knee, in her car seat, in her baby bouncer, and books were propped open beside her changing mat.

About a month later, Rehana began to show a marked preference for books with animals in them, and smiled when the adult sharing the book made the appropriate animal sounds.

When six months old, Rehana began to prefer books with simpler pictures, her two favourites being *Animals* and *Friends,* by Helen Oxenbury. Although attracted to simpler pictures, in common with many other children (Graham, 1991), she rapidly lost interest in those that lacked depth or movement, and those of over-simplified objects heavily outlined in black. Oxenbury's illustrations, although clear and relatively simple, are lively and humorous.

An additional attraction of Helen Oxenbury's books must have been the fact that she could turn the thick board pages, and that the books were small enough for her to hold herself. Larger books, or those with thin paper pages, were a source of frustration to her at this stage.

I decided against giving her any of the fabric books produced for babies, as the illustrations tended to be poor and the storylines non-existent. The books themselves were not aesthetically pleasing, they were floppy, not satisfying to hold, and the pages were difficult to turn. In addition, I did not want to deny Rehana the pleasure of 'proper' books until she was supposedly old enough to treat such books with care. Looking back, I believe that Rehana learnt to handle books at an early age because she had been given real books from the start.

SEVEN TO EIGHT MONTHS

At around the age of seven months, Fiona Pragoff's photo books *How Many?* and *Alphabet* were added to her growing collection of favourite books. It was not merely the brightly coloured, clear photographs that appealed to Rehana. She seemed to enjoy running her fingers over the stiff, smooth, shiny pages and touching and sucking the tactilely interesting spiral ring-bindings. Whilst she continued to enjoy handling these books, it was not long before the pictures began to be of great interest, especially photographs of things within her experience.

Mini board-books, such as Jan Pienkowski's *Colours* and *Zoo,* and a miniature version of Pragoff's *Counting,* became much loved at the age of eight months. Rehana would sit alone holding these small books in her hands, opening and closing them, turning the pages, and turning the books around in her hands. Watching her with these small books, one got the impression that she felt that these were books she could handle independently and enjoy alone.

NINE TO TEN MONTHS

At nine months old, Rehana clearly saw books as a source of pleasure, and also enjoyed the closeness with an adult that came with sharing books. In addition, she showed a developing awareness of how books 'work'. When sharing a book with an adult who turned the pages, she scanned each page while the text was read and the pictures were talked about, and as the page was turned she craned her neck to see what was coming next.

She was introduced to her first 'flap book' and was soon able to operate the flaps of Rod Campbell's *1, 2, 3.*

It seemed to be at around this age that Rehana began to realise that pictures in books have a permanence – that they will remain the same, and always be there when the book is looked at again. It was at this age, too, that she began to make very active choices about the books she was going to look at . She had begun to recognise the covers of the different books. It soon became apparent that when she threw her books off her shelf one by one, it was not always merely for the pleasure of emptying the shelf. Often it was clear that she was making definite choices about which books she wanted to look at. Before each book was discarded she looked at the cover and, once she had found a book she wanted, she would leave the remaining books on the shelf.

Similarly, before bedtime, she enjoyed sharing books with an adult – but if the book chosen by the adult was not to her liking she would push it aside and select another herself, or point to another that the adult had close by. Some books she would want to look at two or three times, others she was happy to look at and listen to once. If she wanted a book again, as we closed the book she would turn it over so that the front was uppermost. If she had had enough of the book, she simply threw it on the floor.

ELEVEN TO TWELVE MONTHS

Since she enjoyed Campbell's counting book, we bought her another by the same author/illustrator. *Look Touch and Feel with Buster* was treated with some caution, as she had never experienced a book which had furry cats which could be stroked or pieces of material that could be lifted up. Rehana enjoyed the feel of books in general and went through a period of ruffling the pages of any book she could get hold of, either an adult's or one of her own.

Rehana would frequently choose a book and hold it out to an adult, and if the adult sat down and started to read it to her she literally curled up with pleasure.

She continued to exercise choice over books to be shared with her and some pictures were clear favourites, so much so that once she had found the picture in the book concerned she often did not bother with the rest of the book.

Since she had first been introduced to Oxenbury's *Animals*, I had repeated the same invented commentary to go with the pictures, and she continued to enjoy this, but she lost interest in the book if it was read by an adult who did not know the 'correct' commentary. When given *Spot Goes to the Farm* by a friend, she immediately knew how to operate the flaps but did not appear to be very interested in the book. About three weeks later, however, and for no apparent reason, this book became one of her favourites, and she would demand that it be read to her repeatedly.

At this age, Rehana began to participate more actively when sharing a book with an adult. If she saw pictures of other furry animals she would gently stroke the picture; if the text gave instructions such as "Let's try to kiss teddy goodnight" she responded by cuddling the adult who was reading to her at the time, or by kissing the teddy in the book.

ONE YEAR

Soon after her first birthday, Rehana was introduced to *Dear Zoo*. She clearly drew on her past experience of books, as she needed no help or encouragement to operate the flaps. Rehana was beginning to enjoy sharing slightly longer books, and quite happily concentrated on the whole of *Dear Zoo*. After the third reading, she knew that the appearance of the puppy coincided with the end of the story and as soon as this page was reached, she turned aside or turned the book over for another reading of it. In an attempt to find her books which had some kind of a story, she was introduced to *Just Like Jasper*. The book is a large paperback, and was not one she could handle easily herself. Initially she was totally uninterested, but once her attention was captured by one picture in the book she happily listened to the story twice and then began to bring this book to an adult to read to her.

Between the ages of twelve and fifteen months, Rehana became an even more active participant when sharing books with an adult. She drew on her past experiences in helping her to make sense of the pictures in books (eg. she pretended to blow out candles on a birthday cake). She also listened very carefully to the text and shook or nodded her head as appropriate, made animal noises, and pointed to parts of her own body if these were mentioned. When first introduced to *Oh Dear*, she enjoyed lifting the flaps but found the story too long. Within ten days she had begun to enjoy the story, and was able to find *Oh Dear* in a pile of story books. By now she obviously knew the story, as she shook her head for each new animal except the last, the hen.

By the age of fourteen months, Rehana enjoyed looking at the background detail in pictures, enjoyed pointing to details she had noticed (eg. an owl on the roof), and also enjoyed looking for specific things suggested by the adult. Following a visit to the countryside during which she saw real horses and peacocks at close range for the first time, the picture of the horse in *Oh Dear* became a favourite, as did the peacock in Ormerod's *Silly Goose*.

When she was fifteen months old, she was given *Baby Goz*. This immediately became a favourite. She confused Goz with a duck – an understandable confusion, given the fact that Goz was very similar to her plastic bath ducks. She made appropriate noises for the cat and dog, knocked on the egg when the words 'knock, knock' were read, and shook her head in response to the question "Are you my mother?". When looking at this book, it became apparent that she had learnt that licking your finger prior to turning a page is something that some readers do when looking at books. Within three days Rehana, was so familiar with this book that she was able to fetch it from a pile of books in another room when asked. Rehana looked at the details in the pictures, was able to point to the tiny butterfly on one page, and knew that the small red smudges on a background of green represented flowers.

A few weeks later, she began to show some interest in *The Very Hungry Caterpillar*. Rehana was fascinated by the double-page spread showing all the food that the caterpillar consumed on Saturday, and would turn to these pages and wait for the adult to name the different foods. At this age the rest of the story was of little consequence. When she first encountered this book, she remembered that another of her books had holes in the pages, and searched for her copy of *Peepo* in order to point out the holes to me.

By the age of sixteen months, Rehana had learnt a lot about the reading process, none of which was taught to her explicitly. It was not surprising therefore, that she had also begun to learn about readers. She had observed adults around her reading books, magazines, letters, lists, notices, the word processing screen, and so on. There are bookshelves full of books in every room in the house, and she had regularly observed her grandmother looking at the books on the shelves, asking questions about new additions to our own collections, and selecting books to borrow. Both parents have books and other reading material in their briefcases, and there are books, magazines, and newspapers on bedside tables and in magazine racks. Not a day passes without Rehana having the opportunity to observe an adult read, and as a result she learnt at a very young age that reading is seen as important and something that the adults in her family enjoy. I had not thought much about how this would be transmitted to Rehana until it struck me that before she was a year old, she had learnt that giving me a book to read was a guaranteed way of getting my immediate and undivided attention. In addition, when going out for the day or in the car, a few of her own books and toys are taken as a matter of course.

From around the age of fourteen months, Rehana began to copy some of the reading behaviours of people. As already observed, she had seen someone licking a finger prior to turning a page, and she too started to do this. She had noticed others studying till receipts, and would copy this behaviour. In a shop she inspected the price labels on clothes, turning them over as she had seen adults around her doing. When playing with her phone, she was no longer content just to dial numbers and 'converse' on the phone, at sixteen months she began to refer to the telephone numbers in a diary prior to 'dialling' the number, sometimes stopping half way through to check the number again.

From a very early age she had also begun to notice who read what. She was used to seeing her grandfather read the newspaper and her grandmother read books, and at around the age of thirteen months would happily hand her grandfather the newspaper but would not give it to her mother or grandmother. She would allow her grandfather to read the newspaper in peace, but not her grandmother. Rehana was, however, quite happy to hand her grandmother the book she had seen her reading. Rehana also noticed the cover of the book, because when her grandmother started a new book Rehana retrieved the old book and tried to insist that her granny read it. Whether one finds social learning theories or cognitive developmental theory more persuasive, Rehana's observations at the age of thirteen months could well lead her to believe that men tend to read newspapers whilst women read books.

Rehana was also learning about the different ways in which the men and women in her family read to her. The men were less confident about sharing books with small children, and had more difficulty in making a book accessible to a very small child. This was evident in the way that they tended to read the text exactly as written or, if the book had no text, were unsure of what to say. Both her father and her grandfather expressed the feeling that they were not very good at reading to Rehana, and it is possible that Rehana sensed their lack of confidence, as she frequently lost interest when they read to her. Her father's skills and confidence rapidly increased, and so too did Rehana's pleasure when he read to her, but her grandfather still feels that he is 'not good at reading to her'.

Research has shown that mothers tend to read more often to infant-aged children than do fathers (eg. Davies and Osmont, 1987; Minns, 1990) and it would be interesting to explore whether this is due to levels of confidence, perceptions of gender roles, or other factors, such as time. Furthermore, it is difficult to know how, if at all, Rehana's early experiences of books and reading would have been different had she been a boy. Would adults have read so much to her? Do adults feel it perfectly 'normal' for a small girl to sit and look at books quietly, but something worthy of comment if a little boy does the same?

When choosing books for Rehana, we have tried to ensure that they present her with a broad selection in terms of authors and illustrators. In addition, we have attempted to ensure that the books chosen for her do not contain stereotypical stories or illustrations, but it has proved surprisingly hard to do this. A prime example is that of finding books that reflect her experiences of grandparents. She would not recognise white haired people in carpet slippers and frilly aprons as grandparents – hers take her swimming, her grandfather cooks, she has never seen her grandmother knit. An audit of her favourite books revealed that only one has a female protagonist and she can be 'just as silly as a goose'!

Given that picture and storybooks not only affirm children's experiences, but also broaden their outlooks (Bender Peterson and Lach, 1990) it is disturbing that so many books for the very young are conforming rather than transforming. On reflection, it is also significant that friends and relations have given her books featuring animals, families and babies, subjects traditionally associated with little girls, whilst, despite the current fashion, she has not been given any books about *Thomas the Tank Engine*, or other 'boys' books.

In conclusion, it would seem clear that small children pick up messages about books and reading at a very early age. Some of the messages are concerned with the pleasure books give, but others relate to people's reading behaviours, many of which seem to be mediated or influenced by gender.

NAIMA BROWNE

Talking to Parents

Julia Hodgeon

"Do I pigeonhole them? If I do, I do it unconsciously. She mothers him. I think is it me, or is it boys?" Russell and Tamsin's mother is trying to compare her son and daughter, to consider, at my invitation, their differing school achievements. Russell is eight, Tamsin seven. Their mother considers that Russell's reading development is only slightly ahead of Tamsin's, but that she reads "with more interpretation... she's more comfortable with reading. He reads to get information, when he reads at all; she reads for pleasure".

For Mark and Emma's parents, the news that, on the whole, girls do better in primary education is a revelation. They are surprised by Emma's confident reading development, because of their experience with her older brother. I explain that gender differences in attainment in reading are well documented, and often occur between members of the same family. They have one question: "Why?"

My efforts to find an answer to this question are part of my history as a teacher, and as a reader. Throughout my long and continuing experience as a classroom teacher, my concern has been with language and learning in early-years education, and with the development of children's reading. By 1980, I had become interested in gender issues as they related to reading. I spent 1982-83 as coordinator of a project sponsored jointly by Cleveland LEA and the Equal Opportunities Commission, examining gender issues in six nursery establishments, where my analysis of written observations revealed socialisation along stereotypical lines. There was clear bias in the curriculum, with girls following the interests of the female adults, and boys pursuing a more independent programme at a distance. There was clear male bias in books and other materials, for example the portrayal of an active male lifestyle, and a passive, observing female one (Hodgeon, 1984).

I soon began to work out a model of reading acquisition, and its relation to gender. My 1983 data showed numerous examples of thoughtful and questioning book-sharing between adults and boys, whilst girls often appeared to be using books as a means to stay near the adult, listening passively. But for boys with little book interest, there was a simple alternative to engaging with reading – they did not select themselves as listeners.

Here was a neat paradox. Boys should have had every advantage in the early acquisition of reading, as they received intensive teacher attention when they did take part in reading activities, and the books available for them to read displayed heavy male bias (Zimet, 1976). By a later stage of schooling, however, many boys were clearly judged less competent in reading, while girls had made significant progress.

Reading attainment was also linked to gender in more measurable ways. For example, in Cleveland in 1983, 70 per cent of references to the Learning Support Service were for males. By 1990, this figure had not substantially changed. Will national assessment at Key Stages offer new measures of the same phenomenon, or provide any novel insights into the gender-related aspects of school achievement?

I was fortunate to be able to carry through my interest in this subject in three later studies. One was observational, working in the infant classrooms of two differing primary schools. But by now it was becoming clear to me that my simplistic views of gender socialisation through reading activities within the classroom would have to be abandoned, in favour of a more complex model, having regard to the centrality of family life and social culture outside the classroom. These two strands formed the basis of the second study, an attempt to assess reading progress by analysing interviews between researcher, parents, teachers, and children. I gained valuable insights from talking to parents and saw that any consideration of reading and gender should include their evidence.

The third study, which is the basis of this article, was based on my own workplace, Bankside, a large primary school with integrated special, needs provision. The sample was small: twelve mainstream children, six boys and six girls, reaching the end of Year 3. The children were matched for age and social background. I interviewed parents, children, and teachers, building a picture of the children as readers from as many viewpoints as possible. I assessed the children's reading, using the *Primary Language Record* Sample Sheet, and matched the results to teachers' own assessments and the Fluency Scale in the *Primary Language Record Handbook*. I found that boys were at least one level of fluency behind girls when assessed in this way. This could not be accounted for in terms of social class, ability, or age.

In this sample, therefore, gender would seem to be the chief determinant of reading fluency at the age of eight. In the search for answers to the question "What makes girls better readers than boys?" four basic areas, which were suggested by my previous research, were investigated:

the effects of gender socialisation at home and at school

the effects of the female culture of the primary school

texts and gender images

reading at home

As the project grew, the words of parents became increasingly interesting, perhaps because theirs is often a neglected voice.

The Effects of Gender Socialisation

at Home and at School

I found the discussion with parents of gender stereotyping related to reading acquisition, not surprisingly, difficult. Attention has to be given here to the school setting in the North East of England, an area traditionally associated with strong gender stereotypes, the home of Andy Capp, with partners referred to warmly as 'our lad' and 'our lass'. Parents agreed that gender stereotyping might be damaging for both sexes. As one mother put it "Next time round I'm going to be a man". Yet both the parents and the teachers I spoke to attempted to defend strong gender roles as 'natural', frequently offering such remarks as "Well, boys are like that" and "I don't think anything about it, that's the way things are".

Most of the parent interviews took place over a hot early summer. As we glanced outside into the street the evidence of strong stereotyping operating as part of the group culture was before our eyes. Large groups of boys would be playing active games whilst girls talked quietly to each other and sometimes sat on the pavement reading stories. Martin's mother was aware that this pattern of play could cause difficulties.

Julia: Do you find difficulty finding time to read to him?

Mother: No. I'd do it anyway, the most difficult thing is trying to
        bring him in off the street to do a bit.

She contrasted Martin's lack of interest in school work with the more secretarial pursuits of his sister.

> Leanne's always been a schooly sort of person, she likes it, she sits at the
> table there reading and writing, they're totally different natured. Martin
> would rather be making things out of Lego, and that sort of thing.

Martin's mother here encapsulates the 'different' attitude with an air of resignation. In contrast, Jenny's mother, who has five children, has a more active view of gender socialisation, which she agrees is harmful to boys' achievements in primary school.

> I think boys when they are primary age are sort of rough and naughty
> and boisterous, because they are brought up to be rough and naughty
> and boisterous and macho, and I think all boys that age are, that's why
> they don't get on in primary.

Carly's mother has two girls, and she is in no doubt that Carly is doing well *because she is a girl*. She argues that, though Carly does like to play outdoors and "has her moments", she

> ...would always sit on your knee with a book, she liked sitting down
> things like drawing and games. Boys seem to spend most of their time

galloping round, they do round here anyway. I think girls are like that and boys are the opposite.

Heath (1983) and Wells (1987) continually link pre-school experience of books with success in learning to read. It is as a way of "disembedding" thinking that the sharing of stories with a more experienced language user is seen as essential. Mothers in my study testified that their girls as very young children "always followed me around" and "never left me". Boys behaved differently. As Russell's mother said, "He would always go off on his own and play with Lego and such, he didn't bother about other people so much". If girls are willing to give more of their companionship to adults, and are more prepared to share books, writing, and other adult-directed play, then it is likely that they will acquire more book experience.

THE EFFECTS OF THE FEMALE CULTURE
ON THE PRIMARY SCHOOL

In Bankside School, parents cannot fail to notice the pattern of male management of a large number of females, which is typical of many primary schools. It is a very simple situation. A large group of women, of whom a substantial number are ancillary workers, are bound into what King (1978) called a "tight but authoritarian atmosphere" by a tiny number of men. Most parents I have interviewed or spoken to informally do not find this strange. Many report children's experience of receiving attention from the male head or deputy warmly. "Andrew was thrilled when Mr. B. heard him read." "Kirsty likes Assembly when Mr. S. takes it." "Martin came home today and said Mr. S. had been teaching them, really chuffed he was."

Parents and children are less familiar with a male presence in the normal classroom. Neither the head or deputy has any teaching commitment (Martin's experience was rare), and so the children see them both as only authority figures, or the person who tells a story in assembly. Even the Reception class is in no doubt as to their right to rule, however. "Mr. S. is really the boss of all of you" said one five-year-old boy recently. In many interviews, parents thought that boys who give trouble in school 'needed a man'. More importantly, it is likely that the lack of close contact with male role models at a more everyday level, such as male readers in the classroom, gives the reading process (and with it the whole schooling process) the air of a feminine sphere of influence, and that of a lowly kind in the eyes of the boys. And the boys' view of reading as a female activity is reflected in the expectations of the teachers, which have long been known to influence attainment in the classroom

(Tizard et al, 1988). Teachers expected boys to cope less well with reading, as in fact they were doing, and girls to be good readers, as in fact they were proving to be.

Parents had sometimes had teachers express these expectations directly to them, often to their indignation.

> I think it would do Robert a world of good to be with somebody else. Mrs. R. told me she didn't think he would catch up with his reading, they don't get on, he isn't, well, he isn't well behaved. She's always looking for something he's done.

Failures in personal relationships between children, teachers, and parents are commoner than is often supposed. Parents sometimes expressed their own difficulties in relating to schools in terms of a child's dislike and hostility. Such situations were as common with girls as boys, and were bound up with expectations of success and failure. Paradoxically, it is sometimes quiet, achieving girls whom adults perceive as difficult in the classroom. The child who never says 'boo to a goose' may be seen by her teacher as more irritating than a noisy, troublesome boy whose 'heart is in the right place'. By erecting stereotypes in this way, teachers may encourage children to reinforce their learned behaviour, and thus their self-image as readers.

TEXTS AND GENDER IMAGES

In interviews with parents I tried to explore the mystery of why male bias in texts does not appear to affect reading attainment, since it seems neither to encourage boys nor discourage girls. With changes in publishing policies, bias is now becoming more difficult to find, and distinctions are much more blurred. This applies to texts published in the last ten years, where older criteria, such as counting the numbers of male and female characters, are becoming out of date. However there are still clear gender-related preferences which parents report in children's reading. Boys were fond of comics, which still exhibit strong gender bias – for example, those with semi-scientific themes, 'themes of violence and terror', as White (1990) calls them. Girls liked comics with themes of social caring and negotiation, as well as those based on the pop culture. Parents did not discourage comics, but drew the line at reading them aloud. They looked on them as part of children's culture, a separate world.

Barrs and Pidgeon (1980) pointed out that there were few pictorial or descriptive images in books of persons actually reading. Such images are now far more common, and include males reading to babies and children. I found that parents did not seek out books with such images, and there was some evidence that they found the need for the provision of

suitable materials puzzling. Perhaps the provision of a non-sexist book-list could help parents in this way. A short list of this kind could be compiled by teachers with their own school's parents in mind, and could accompanied by a straightforward rationale expressed in clear terms. The list could be used when parents and children went shopping for presents, or as a request list for birthdays and Christmas. It is easy to underestimate parents' own views in this area. They offered thoughtful theories, and sometimes went back to their children's reading matter to check what we had discussed. One such mother offered the following:

> I think it doesn't make a lot of difference what you have in the books. Girls will read most things anyway because they're used to accepting things. Boys won't have what they think is women's stuff.

READING EXPERIENCES AT HOME

All the children I interviewed owned reading materials. Parents willingly confirmed this, and showed me amounts varying from a few to many books, which were sometimes shared by the family. All the children used the school lending service to some extent. However, *whatever the reading competency of the child*, by the age of eight, parents had largely stopped reading to them. Only one parent in the sample said her child was still hearing stories from both parents, her sister, and her grandmother. All other parents considered that the child could manage alone, being a 'good little reader', or that tuition, in the form of hearing the child read, had assumed greater urgency. The bedtime story seemed to have ceased when the child assumed greater responsibility for going to bed alone.

Book sharing was available to the children in other ways. None of them were singletons. All except two of them spoke warmly of sharing books with older or younger siblings. Foreman and Cazdan (1985) emphasise the importance of these reading partnerships in terms of the equality of the teaching and learning relationships which they generate. They may sometimes provide the only experience of being read to in the home available to the children.

There were differential effects of the *same* experience. Most parents I talked to had stopped reading to their children by the time when I was interviewing them. Given the competence of the girls, and their evident willingness to explore more complex texts, for example Samantha's liking for 'chapter books', the effects on them might not be serious. However, boys were being treated *as if they had similar competence*, even when they were not able to read with independence. More complex texts with involved narratives might usefully have carried them forward.

Parents had a conviction that their children either *could* or *couldn't* read. They prioritised their time to hear smaller ones read and help those in difficulty, and since most were at least part-time workers that was likely to be that. One mother, part of a family with an extensive reading culture, though one of the poorest in material terms, was sure that this was the right approach.

Julia: Do you read to him now?

Mother: Oh no Julia, I think it's a lot nicer when they read to you.

There is some evidence here that parents, after pre-school and initial school experience, have given over the reading task to the school. In a sense, they feel they have done their bit. The close cooperation stressed by teachers of young children begins to fade. Much evidence, however, for example Tizard et al, (1988), suggests that continued cooperation would boost achievement.

In important ways, the reading experience of girls and boys did differ in the home. By the age of eight, girls in the sample initiated and sustained their own reading. Their motivation as readers was well established. They had all succeeded in achieving some kind of independence, largely as a result of past support at home and at school (Minns, 1990). On arriving home from school, or in spare moments later, they read alone, and gained pleasure from doing so. Parents described them as "always having her head in a book", "being well away with it", and as "good little readers". They seemed to ask for little adult support.

Boys had a different experience. Their book reading experiences at home were likely to be adult-initiated. Martin's mother had difficulty in "getting him in off the street to do a bit". Graeme's mother said that "We do more reading in the winter-time, he's not playing out then". They read aloud to adults, usually the mother or an older sibling, since fathers were described as "having no patience with him", or "always losing his temper". Parental anxiety, now becoming acute in some cases, ensured that adults were prepared to spend time for overtly tutorial purposes. "I know he can't have enough individual attention at school, so I'll do it at home", "I'll do it if it kills me", were two remarks which indicated extremes of the same position.

WORKING TOGETHER

Perhaps the most disturbing feature of my interviews was parents' lack of knowledge about the effects of a child's gender on success and failure in primary schooling. Reluctance to discuss the issue was particularly noticeable amongst fathers. Although many interviews took place in the presence of both partners, and all were the children's natural parents, I have no record of any male comment, other than to express surprise or recount their own reading history. The questions of "Why?" and "What should be done about it?" were always answered by mothers. There is a hint here at primary schooling as a female domain, and reading as a female pre-occupation.

This seems to me one of the keys to changing attitudes. For it to work, male carers, whether parents or teachers, would need to cooperate with their partners and colleagues, firstly, in acquiring the necessary knowledge about what needs to be done, and secondly, acting on the situation through a set of conscious strategies. If, as a quarter of the male adult sample told me, they had been put off reading for life by their own primary school experiences, it is surely reasonable to suppose that they should not want the same experiences for their own children.

Such strong parental motivation might provide the basis for a way forward. There are some misconceptions about reading as part of a developmental strand of education. Parents tend to see reading acquisition as a once and for all dose, not as a foundation for lifetime development. Their support (and particularly the support of male carers), must be encouraged to continue beyond the first two years of the primary school, and take the form of reading to, as well as reading with, both girls and boys.

Teacher expectations are crucial here. It is easy for them to transfer such expectations, based on gender stereotypes, to parents. Mental sets such as "His reading is OK for a boy" or "Not very advanced for a girl" are sometimes implicit in teachers' discussions of progress in the primary school. Such attitudes do children little service when they are sensed and absorbed by parents. A more thoughtful and explicit sharing, by contrast, might improve the confidence, knowledge, and self-image of both parents and children.

In their homes, most children were using a wide range of reading materials, including comics and hobby magazines, the latter often shared with fathers. Provision in school of such materials might not only sometimes lead to fruitful discussion of gender stereotypes with children, but would also stress the links between home and school, which are essential if every child is to be given an equal opportunity to become a literate and thinking being.

JULIA HODGEON

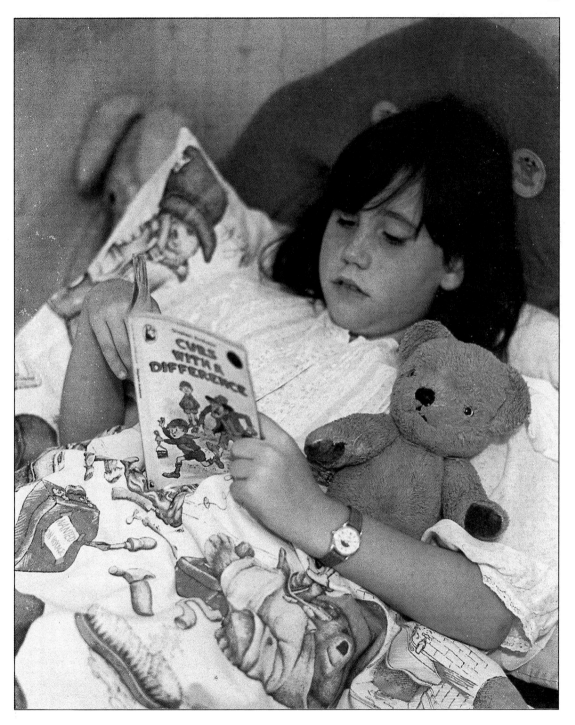

Three Ten-Year-Old Boys
and their Reading

HILARY MINNS

Over the last twenty years or so the relationship between gender, language, and learning has been explored in different curricular areas. In 1984, the APU Primary Language Survey looked at children's reading patterns, and included a gender dimension in its findings. The results showed that, on the whole, boys read more slowly than girls, and that girls prefer to read fiction, while boys prefer information books.

But since each child has a unique reading biography, how did the survey account for any differences it might have found within, as well as across, the sexes? And were all the important aspects of boys' and girls' reading patterns documented by the researchers? Margaret Meek Spencer, (1983) commenting on the survey *Children and their Books* (Whitehead, 1977), noted that:

> Many boys have views of reading we never hear about because most of what they read is passed over as insignificant

I decided to look specifically at the reading patterns and preferences of three ten-year-old boys – Clayton, Gurdeep, and Simon – to try and discover more about their reading. Working with children of the same sex would enable me to focus more closely on what the influences might be for one group; from this I could perhaps make tentative suggestions about both boys' and girls' reading choices.

There were deliberate reasons for choosing these three particular boys. I taught Clayton several years ago, and still have tapes of our conversations; his reading life fascinated me then and continues to do so now. I worked with Gurdeep and his family five years ago, as part of an earlier research project. I knew him well as a beginning reader, and was curious to know how his reading had developed over the five years, and how much Sikhism would continue to influence his literacy practices. Simon, who goes to the same school as Gurdeep, has always interested me, because he has never conformed to any stereotyped behaviour patterns, and I wanted to see how this might have affected his reading choices and responses.

All three boys have experience of reading for their own pleasure, and it is worth noting that the school Gurdeep and Simon go to, and the school where I taught Clayton, both had reading policies that were distinguished by the way in which they highlighted the importance of literature as a basis for learning to read. In addition, from the beginning of schooling, the boys were expected to exercise choice in their reading. Their reading satisfaction, their desire to read, has always been encouraged; they saw themselves as authors of books that were read by others in their class.

CLAYTON

Readers of Donald Fry's book *Children Talk About Books: Children Seeing Themselves as Readers* and my article in *Alice in Genderland*, 'Girls don't get holes in their clothes' will already have met Clayton. They will know him as a boy who came slowly to value fiction in his life but, having once been captivated by the power of story, did not want to let it go. They might also remember Clayton's spirited defence of the boys' controlled response to Charlotte's death in *Charlotte's Web*, when we read and discussed the story in class.

I interviewed Clayton when he was ten, and no longer in my class, to see where his reading had taken him during the year. I wondered if he would still be exploring the world of literature, searching out books where animals figure powerfully as central characters, or possibly reading other books by E.B. White, Richard Adams, or Raymond Briggs. I expected him to still be following his farming interests. This is what he said:

Clayton: I've read *Dragonfall Five and the Space Cowboys*, *Dragonfall Five and the Hijackers* and *Charlotte's Web* twice this year and I've read *Angler's Mail*. I've read the Robin Hood book I've got at home. And there's a space book. I've read that a couple of times...and I read the 'Farmer's Weekly' that I have posted for me...I get 'Pig Farm Management' and 'Arable Farming' as well...I have a comic as well. I have one of those every week.

Hilary: Is the 'Farmer's Weekly' yours or your dad's?

Clayton: Mine. I get my own package. He goes and buys his.

Hilary: Why do you need your own copies?

Clayton: Cos he likes to cut things out of his...you can see all the details. How much the price has gone up from pigs say about last year and pigs this year...

A picture of Clayton's reading begins to emerge. He has re-read *Charlotte's Web*, the book that is so important to him. His interest in action-based narrative and the world of fantasy is there too; yet there is no hint that he is reading books of quality in this area – he makes no mention of Ursula le Guin or Ray Bradbury. His farming interests are plainly evident too, and he reads to help him become a good farmer alongside his father.

Clayton is consciously shaping his reading life to meet the demands his present and future roles are making on him. The family now has its own riding stables and Clayton is reading 'a lot more horse books.' I ask him if these are information books or story books:

Information books. Shows you diagram of the body and all the things that they have and all that lot, how to cut them properly and pick their feet properly with a hoof pick. It shows you all that you need.

Clayton realises that much of what he needs to know lies between the pages of information books and specialist magazines. Yet how, as a reader of fiction, does he cope with the transition to this kind of reading material?

> Well, it is different not reading so many story books, cos story books are much easier cos...cos the the information books, erm, they take a long time to read for a start, and most of the times you can't understand the words that are in them. The story books, some are easy, some hard, and you can get the words right. I read with my dad, so if I get any words wrong I learn them on a piece of paper...erm...still, I like information books as well, cos the information in the pictures is what I go for.

I suspect that Clayton learns most of his farming techniques from actual experience and uses the books to authenticate this specialist knowledge, to give it status: a way of making sense of the world of farming that puts him closer to his father. I ask him if there will ever be a time when he won't read story books:

> No. I'll always read story books...I'll never finish with story books, cos for the past six years I've read about 700 books, different, all different books, and about 300 all the same books over and over again.

He records his reading carefully so that "when I grow up, if I have children I can show them the good books".

Clayton takes his reading seriously, and chooses to read things that are important to him. He seems set to follow his father's farming interests, and some of his reading closely mirrors that of his father. Clayton is a reader who picks up information about the world from many sources, and who remembers what he's read.

Certain fictions in his reading life are returned to over and over again. *The Snowman* and *Watership Down* have been two important texts in his life and Donald Fry noted particularly the way Clayton and his father read and enjoyed *Watership Down* together.

> Clayton 'watches' the book as his father reads. "He reads one chapter and then I go over it before we go to bed every night"...In Clayton's home there are books about trains, farming, horses and wildflowers. His father becomes interested himself in *Watership Down* and asks if he can borrow it, and, says Clayton, moans because there is not enough quiet. Thus Clayton sees his interest in the book confirmed by his father, and maintained by the regular readings, which, having read ahead, his father does well: Clayton particularly liked the different noises he made for the rabbits. (Fry, 1988).

It was perhaps through *Watership Down* especially that Clayton came to a closer understanding of himself as a reader and a person. Another book which has influenced him dramatically is *Charlotte's Web*. He has read it "twice this year", and he certainly read it more than once when he was in my class. Not surprisingly, perhaps, it is another book which relates to the countryside, to farmers, and to farming. His public response to parts of the book, from our class discussion, was documented in *Alice in Genderland*:

> Julia: Miss it was very sad when Charlotte died. I... everyone, nearly everyone cried.
> Clayton: Only the boys didn't cry cos they were brill.
> Boys: Yeah.
> David: True, Clayton.
> Clayton: We don't cry like girls. They're babies.
> Boys: True.

There seems to be clear pressure on Clayton to perform this way in the group and his views are supported by many of the boys. He stereotypes himself as he plays the 'tough-guy' role. However, when I talked to him on his own, his response was different. Without an audience it became possible for him to think himself more deeply into the book.

> Clayton: I wonder how old Charlotte was, if she was there before all that.
> Hilary: Yes, now that's something that it doesn't tell us. I wonder how long she had been there.

Clayton interwove his interest in Charlotte with his knowledge about the life of spiders:

> At the end of the book she prob...well they live, they live, to...they start – they start – they come out erm about February, March, something like that, and they grow up to, say, November early December, cos in the December they would have died anyway, cos it would have been too cold and no good because all the flies stay in then and they're dead anyway.

Clayton has strong feelings about this book, but having feelings and being able to put them into words are very different things. Perhaps some boys are less likely to express their feelings than girls; perhaps, too there is a difference between what boys feel and what they say they feel. On this occasion, Clayton chooses to interrogate the text in a way which keeps his feet securely in the world of facts as he discusses the life expectancy of spiders. Although he reflects on the story and the characters he also demonstrates here his characteristic stance towards text: looking firmly outward, away from himself.

Rosenblatt (1978) describes two functions of reading, which she characterises as 'efferent' and 'aesthetic'. Efferent reading is reading of a factual nature, for a specific purpose; aesthetic reading is about reading with desire and pleasure. It is as if Clayton is transforming what could be a totally aesthetic experience into a factual exchange of dates, and making them part of his theory of how the world works.

Clayton's sense of himself as a reader appears to be related to his own developing masculine identity. Two things are of key importance to him: his father and the world of farming. They are the pivot on which his life turns, and, although he demonstrates a sensitive response to fiction, at the same time he feels pressured to construct a stereotyped masculine role in his public response, often on his guard against certain ways of reading and responding, and asserting other ways time and time again.

GURDEEP

Readers might have met Gurdeep in Chapter 1 of *Read It To Me Now!* At four-and-a-half, he was interested in picture-story books and fairy tales, 'Transformers', and adverts on the television, and was also learning a great deal about his family's cultural and religious traditions.

As a young boy, Gurdeep listened to his mother as she read the *Guru Granth Saheb* in Panjabi, and he heard the holy book read by the priest at the Temple. His mother used to tell him fables she heard as a girl in India; Gurdeep's father read him bedtime stories, sometimes Indian stories written in English or a dual-text Panjabi-English story, "so that they know their own culture, the background".

When Gurdeep was seven he was reading independently and choosing his own books from the local library. At this time he had begun to learn Panjabi at the temple. He liked writing on his computer and watching popular TV shows. Gurdeep was becoming immersed in the literacy activities of two cultures.

At ten years old, Gurdeep hears his mother saying that "as he's a boy he's got less interest in reading. He reads some but he likes riding his bike or watching television. If you don't know what programme is coming on the television, ask Gurdeep! He'll tell you this film is coming on at this time and it's going to be good."

At school Gurdeep reads story books – "funny stories and stories by Roald Dahl, like *Matilda*." He says he doesn't read many information books, except when he has to do research for a project: "At the moment I'm doing snakes. What sort of things they eat. The names. I know how to tell snakes from each other, like the milk snake and the coral snake."

Gurdeep is very interested in the structure of language, possibly because his growing knowledge of Panjabi gives him a way of studying English.

> Me and my friend read dictionaries, like *The Concise Oxford Dictionary*. We have races to find things in a dictionary. I'm used to finding all the letters, the capitals, and all that. In Panjabi, there are new words that I learn when I translate them into English. I've never heard of them before, and I find the meanings and I learn new words as well.

Gurdeep's knowledge of the world is extending daily as he learns how to become a good citizen and upholder of the morality, truth, and justice of the Sikh religion. The words of the *Guru Granth Saheb* are deep within his daily act of worship, his music-making, and his religious observance. As well as the importance for him of home and school, the temple is the centre of his learning life and his place of worship. He goes there once a week to learn to read and write Panjabi, and to play the drums. There are two boys and eight girls in his Panjabi group. "It seems like the boys aren't interested", he observes.

As soon as Gurdeep can read Panjabi well enough, he will start prayer classes at the temple to study the *Guru Granth Saheb*, "but you have to learn how to read it first".

Like other Sikh boys, Gurdeep is learning to play the drums at the temple.He has been studying different rhythms for ten months, and he has written these down to help him remember them. Gurdeep reads this language of musical rhythm quite precisely, and he accompanies his sister on the harmonium, and she sings prayers from the holy books. They practice together each evening and have already performed at the temple with other children. This musical tradition, and its accompanying literacy, is specifically rooted in the religious and cultural traditions of Gurdeep's family and community. It is also gender-related, since boys learn the tabla, and is therefore part of Gurdeep's growing identity as a Sikh male. Gurdeep has a cousin who is a professional tabla player and has appeared on television.

Gurdeep is an acknowledged good reader at school, and talks, quite matter-of-factly, about the way his male friends follow what he does:

> Some of my friends start reading what I read, cos I'm the best reader in the upper school. If I've got a book and I've just finished reading it, they ask if they can read it next. They always do what I do, and they play what I play.

He still has his comic collection at home. He collected Turtles comics every week two years ago and points to the pile. "I was into Brave Star. All my friends and everyone." He adds that "mum and dad always tell me off if they catch me reading comics. They say it's got all this slang language in." Nevertheless, he is captivated by adventurous and fantastic characters, and uses comics, stories and television programmes to enter their worlds.

Gurdeep reads parts of the local free newspaper His favourite thing to do is to "just look at things for sale in the 'Miscellaneous' to see if there's anything interesting that's cheap that I could buy with my own money." He reads the front page in the 'Daily Mail' "where it says the headline, or sometimes if there's something about tennis or cricket results, I'll read that as well." He gets Asterix books from the library and describes *The Adventures of Asterix* with great enthusiasm:

> It's about a little Gaulish village in the centre of Compendium and they're on an island and on the other side of the island there's a Roman camp and the hero is Asterix and they have to fight the Romans...They have silly names like the chief of the Gaulist village is called Vitalstatistix and there's Obelix and Getafix.'

Gurdeep's most recent library book is *The Crimson Tide*, one of the *Fighting Fantasy* series. He chose it because it puts him at the heart of an exciting adventure, as demonstrated by the blurb: Arcane creatures, martial monks and battle-hardened warriors must all be overcome, as your quest for justice leads you from your quiet village to the very Court of the God-King!

This book and others in the series aren't available at school. It is the first one of the series that Gurdeep has chosen, and he's having difficulty getting to the end of the adventure, because he constantly meets foes who defeat him on his journey to the Court.

His father reads books on technology and engineering, and Gurdeep observes that

> he needs it cos he does wiring, he makes circuit boards at work. I read some of them as well. Some of them have got words I've never heard of. I don't read them, I go away and get another book.

This confidence to choose *not* to read a particular book comes, I believe, from his being invited to choose what to read, as well as what not to read, from the beginning of his time in school. Margaret Meek writes of those more experienced readers who:

> ...do not know reading as easy or difficult; they scarcely distinguish adults' books from children's books. They see books as good or bad, in the first instance, as what gives, or does not give them pleasure. They divide books into boring or not boring; the boring ones they leave, the others they read to the end.

Gurdeep has an enormously wide range of literacies, both in Panjabi and English. Of note, too, is his interest in language itself, and the differences between his two languages. But despite its breadth, Gurdeep's preferred reading in English has certain marked characteristics. Perhaps this is linked to his television viewing and reading of comics - he particularly likes books in a comic format, like Asterix, books that are influenced by computer technology, like *The Crimson Tide*, and other graphic novels: these are all texts with a strong visual content. He favours funny stories and Roald Dahl books.

Gurdeep's reading is related to his peer group membership, and to his sense of what his friends are doing: his computer literacy and television literacy are part of this world. In these ways he is a recognisable male reader; the fictional worlds he chooses to enter are action worlds, and he consumes them fast and expertly, quickly learning how to read new genres.

SIMON

Simon's mother said she "just did what came naturally" when she brought him up as a baby.

> I didn't do things just cos everyone else did. I didn't conform. If Simon wanted dolls or cuddly toys he had them. He sometimes used to dress up in my shoes!

She says she wouldn't have brought a girl up differently. Simon says:

> I just had normal soft toys and teddy bears and books. There's nothing babyish about a teddy bear. I had just one gun. My favourite toy was a big yellow teapot. I've got a lot of Lego.

Simon can't remember how he learnt to read but his mother says, "He's always had books. First he had a cloth book and then a book for his bath, then hard-backed books".

Simon's mother doesn't really enjoy reading, though she sometimes reads short stories – "I like short sharp shocks!" She reads complicated knitting machine and tapestry patterns. In contrast, his father likes to read on his own, and will take himself off with a book, something that Simon has "got off his dad". In spite of having to work away from home for long periods, Simon's father is a powerful influence in his reading life, and Simon's most treasured possession is the cased set of *Narnia* books which his father bought him.

Simon's father reads golf and fishing magazines, and westerns. "If he takes up a hobby the books will come," says his wife. Simon's father makes the most of his time at home to follow his interests in golf and fishing, and he plays golf with Simon.

When Simon was little his father used to make up stories to tell him. Now, Simon enjoys reading adventure and fantasy – "I'll read anything that's got adventure in," he says. He likes funny stories too. "I like Michael Rosen, but I've gone off Roald Dahl because some of his stories are a bit boring." Interestingly, he has no time for the kind of adventure books that Gurdeep is reading. "It's just a game really. You play the book!" He also collects pop and show-biz comics like 'Fast Forward' and 'Smash Hits' avidly, and is knowledgeable about current stars, both male and female.

Simon reads parts of 'The Sun' and the 'News of the World'. "I mostly read what the article is about, and if I like it I read it again. If it's a bit boring I just turn over to the next page. Most of the stories are sad but I just read them." Sometimes he reads interesting articles aloud to his parents.

At school Simon plays with both boys and girls, and he enjoys girls' company. "I don't know why. I just do. They're more sensible than boys cos most boys fight." He has thought deeply about gender differences:

> Mostly, we do mixed things. We just don't think about the boys being boys and the girls being girls, we just do things together. That's it really. We used to line up in separate lines but we don't any more because most of the boys and girls think it's sexist.

Simon's comments on gender roles are perhaps unusual for a boy of his age, and it is interesting to speculate on how his democratic view of gender roles has influenced his view of reading generally – he certainly chooses reading material that feels right for him as a person. Reading is part of his life, and I recall his mother's words about his father going off and reading on his own when Simon tells me:

> When I go upstairs, I always take a book up and then I read it. I just want to be on my own to read. I can just sit down with three or four books and read.

Simon has the strong feel of an experienced reader about him. He knows what he likes to read, and he knows how to read different texts, such as newspapers and novels, in different ways.

Simon showed me his prized boxed *Narnia* series. "I like to collect a series of books," says Simon, "because you can read the follow-up, and it's like a big event that's happened. Each single book is like a fantasy...I feel I'm in a strange and magical world." His favourite book in the series is *The Lion, The Witch and the Wardrobe,* which he's read "at least twenty times". Simon shows how he is becoming a discerning reader when he begins to talk about the difficult area of stories which reflect and illuminate life. For Simon a 'character' in a story is someone who has nice things happen to them; but a story with 'real people' in dares to show that life isn't always like that:

> I don't like happy endings, as it never happens to us most of the time. The girls from *The BFG* – she's like a real person, not like a character. You can't predict what the future's going to be for you, but you can with a book because you can just read it again and again.

As Simon enters the world of the book, he reflects on the relationship between literature and life. He knows that the ending of a book can never change, and takes security and satisfaction from this; at the same time he uses literature, with its safe story-world, to help him to understand the uncertainties of the human condition. His constant re-reading is part of this process of response. Simon reflects on the importance of characters in stories and explains:

> I suppose I don't take sides over whether they should have done this or they should have done that – I just think about it as real life and just pretend·that...like...that they're not actually a character in a book, they're a real person and they always have to do things...I just take it normally really.

Like Clayton, Simon is a reader who holds certain books dear to him. Unlike Clayton, he seems at all times prepared to look inside himself and to consider his own response, and how he reads, stating his own feelings with conviction. Where Clayton takes himself out of the book and back into the safe world of facts and farming, Simon is prepared to dwell inside the text and ponder on the relation of text to life. At the same time, he is a thoroughly ordinary pre-teenager in his interest in pop and in the 'News of the World'.

So is there anything that can be learned about gender-related reading from these three boys, even though each boy's reading pattern is unique, and deeply centred within both the cultural traditions of family and community and the wider media culture?

To some extent, what underpins the focus of the boys' reading choices, most particularly for Clayton and Simon, is the influence of their fathers. The boys, consciously or otherwise, model some of their own reading behaviour on their fathers' particular reading styles and preferences. Perhaps their response to books, the kind of reader they are becoming, is closely related to their view of their fathers as readers. If so, this must surely raise questions about the reading patterns of boys who do not see their fathers read, or boys who are brought up by their mothers alone. And what of boys who are taught exclusively by female teachers all the way through their nursery and primary schools?

Perhaps only Simon, with his significant literary expertise, and his ability to inhabit the world of the text, can truly explore his own response and look inwards at the emotional experience of fiction: he knows that these things are possible. In Gurdeep's case, his male friends at school seem to be the strongest influence on his reading in English – this is perhaps not so surprising, since school is the place where Gurdeep encounters many English stories and novels, and also the place where he discusses current media interests with friends of his own age.

It is worth speculating about the areas of literacy encountered by the boys which are most likely to be gender-related: certainly computer texts, farming magazines, adventure comics and books, fighting-fantasy books, and the sports pages in newspapers come to mind. If I had chosen to work with three girls, would their reading practices have been different? Books by Roald Dahl and the *Narnia* series would probably figure prominently in their reading, but would there be so much reading of newspapers and fantasy books? Would the comics they chose be ones written specially to appeal to girls? If so, why should this be? Their choices would almost certainly be influenced by the media, as are those of the boys, but their particular experiences and life expectations, interwoven as they are within their complex networking of friendships, would probably encourage different reading needs and choices for girls. In addition to this, how significant for girls is the reading pattern of their mothers, and the influence of female teachers?

Clayton, Gurdeep, and Simon are already looking outward, towards the grown-up world, as they seek to increase their respective knowledge of farming, Sikhism, the Panjabi language, and the world of literature. Interestingly, many of the texts they read, such as Panjabi texts, farming magazines, newspapers and pop magazines, do not appear to be part of their reading experience in school, yet are vitally important to them. Margaret Meek identified this issue as a problem some years ago. It is surely time now for schools to validate this reading, so that boys can identify themselves as competent readers of a variety of texts.

All three boys are learning what it is to be male and to be readers, and these two areas are inextricably linked. Teaching a boy to become a reader, and to remain a reader, involves helping him to develop a reading identity that offers him a way of being a male, and which at the same time encourages him to develop a personal response – possibly at the risk of being different.

HILARY MINNS

TEXTS

Gender Wars

Lissa Paul

GENDER WARS AT HOME

What is a five year old girl to do at a large family party when a pair of five year old boys won't play with her, because, they say, girls aren't tough enough to play Batman? Even though they've all seen the movie, and know perfectly well that Catwoman is a good match for the man in black.

The girl retreated to the art table and began cutting paper. The boys received a lecture on gender relations from me (the party was at my house, and one of the boys is my son). They were reminded that among their own mothers, grandmothers, and aunts are lawyers, a judge, engineers and a professor. They were also reminded that in both their families mothers and fathers worked, cared for the children, and did domestic work. And they were reminded that toughness was not a necessarily desirable commodity, but even on the assumption that it was desirable, their own mothers displayed 'toughness' in spades. They would have apologized to the girl, but she had left by the time the lecture was over.

As a feminist mother and a feminist teacher I was distressed by the incident (you can tell from the way I've rendered it in the passive), even though I know all too well that gender politics are alive and well in the day care and in the kindergarten and in the playground – and at my house. Boys exclude girls because they are not 'tough' enough, and because they play with dolls and not trucks. The scenario itself is not too surprising, and I would guess that anyone reading this would recognize it instantly – from either the male or female perspective – as something typical of their own childhoods.

The girl at my party quietly retreated, a tactic I recognized instantly as typical of girls, and one I regret using myself more often than I'd like to confess. The problem with girls (little or big) using retreat as a survival tactic is that boys (little or big) remain secure in their dominance: their toys, games, books and interests remain the desirable ones. Girls are, at best, tolerated. According to little boys, dolls are generally low on the play scale of desirability.

I did come up with a way to disturb that value system with my own children. When my sons began to play with Batman models (the older equivalent was GI Joe), I innocently asked if they enjoyed playing with their Batman dolls. Their shocked, slightly guilty expressions belied their verbal protests; they knew the comparison was just. And lately I haven't heard any derogatory remarks about dolls.

GENDER WARS AT SCHOOL

Things are supposed to be different now. The Ontario Ministry of Education (I'm writing from Toronto, though I expect similar guidelines on gender bias are in place in Europe and elsewhere in North America) has had a policy on sex-role stereotyping since 1978. That translates as a whole generation of school children who should have learned that sexual discrimination is as bad for their social and psychological health as smoking is for their physical health. The policy states that teachers should "ensure that the stories used with children *portray* girls and boys and women and men in a variety of positive *active* roles" (emphasis mine). Two things worry me; the preference for pictures over discussion; and the *privileging of activity*.

We've turned issues of gender equity into a kind of dumb show, thinking it enough to show pictures of smiling lady fire fighters (note the correct gender neutral term) while eliding the issue of who is looking after the kids at home when she is on call at the fire station. Her husband? And what happens when she's pregnant?

We've also created a generically ideal audience for these pictures, as Valerie Walkerdine says in *Schoolgirl Fictions*. We've created the "universal child", "gender-neutral, self-disciplined, and active". Activity is still privileged, and so the subtle preference for the male term prevails. No wonder the politics of the playground still sound much as I remember them. Real children aren't gender neutral. Neither are their parents. Static images, as Valerie Walkerdine suggests, often set up "hidden conflicts", and these are the ones we are just beginning to explore. Images of masculinity and femininity are not static. They are, as she says, "struggled over in a complex relational dynamic". That's what we're looking for when choosing texts for children.

In *Piggybook*, by Anthony Browne, the 'complex relational dynamic' appears to be missing. Though the book looks like it is about relative values of work, the work is assigned in split shifts rather than struggles. Daddy and the boys are male chauvinist piggies when they let mummy do the work at the beginning of the story. Even after they learn their lessons at the end of the book, the three little piggies stick together sharing the cooking while mummy appears on her own in a separate frame fixing the car. Though she is bowed down and drab in the first housework sequences, and smiling a dirty-faced smile while she fixes the car, she still works alone while the boys work together. One of my colleagues, Pam Nason, a specialist in early childhood education, suggests that Browne offers the image as a kind of joke. I hadn't thought of the possibility until she suggested it, but I try to read Browne's book that way now, and try to explore the tantalizing possibilities of irony. Pam's comment about the story, our conversations about it, enabled me to see a complex relational dynamic in the book that I hadn't recognized before. That conversation is, it seems to me, where the struggles take place. They are exactly the kinds of conversations advocated in contemporary ideas about literary discourse. Aidan Chambers calls them book-talks.

TALES OUT OF SCHOOL

As a feminist mother of two sons, both on the verge of entering the school system, I'm sensitive to the nuances of gender wars, and constantly sobered by my own experience. From the age of eighteen months, my older son Matthew, now five, gravitated to the transportation section at our local children's book store, though he reads and knows a wide range of fiction and poetry (as would be expected of a child with a parent in the field). When he heads for the transportation section, I don't flinch any more. I know he knows the keys to literacy are in the discourse not the static image. A story he dictated to me when he was four and a half, 'Construction sites and Other Machines', provides a hint. Here is his text for the first spread:

A Medium-Sized Backhoe

The backhoe is digging a trench for the pipe to
go through and come out the other end and then
it will be digging in other stories. There will
be another of these so look out for it.

I know Matthew is patterning this story after one of his construction books, *Monster Road Builders*. I also know that he has picked up (probably not from *Monster Road Builders* but from one of the 'literary' books we read him) the idea that literary texts have patterns in them, and that readers and writers look for patterns. Not a specifically gendered observation, I know, but it is certainly a literary one. He understands that literature isn't static or silent, and that the patterns in the text enable him to articulate his feelings and his sense of himself in relation to the world.

Another bit of anecdotal evidence provides a clue. At four, during his first weeks in Junior Kindergarten (the reception class), Matthew suddenly refused to go to gym class. He had apparently become terrified by the gym instructor, who was more at home with boisterous ten-year-old boys. When asked directly why he was afraid, Matthew could only say it was because the teacher " was as loud as giants stomping on the land". He understood the metaphors necessary to express his own sense of being victimized. In conversation he also understood that, although he couldn't kick a giant in the shins to any good effect, he certainly could ask the giant "to speak nicely to children". Again, he understood the discourse.

MAKING A DIFFERENCE

I know my comments have been personal so far, with only slight references to specific texts, so I'd like to turn now to the subtle way gender relations are threaded into the ideological discourse in a recent picture book for children, *Farmer Duck*, by Martin Waddell and Helen Oxenbury.

Farmer Duck is a kind of Orwellian *Animal Farm* for the pre-school set, a Marxist primer for a post-Marxist age. A male duck is slave to male farmer. Most of the time, the duck is referred to generically as 'duck'. It is not until the third page from the end that the duck is acknowledged as male – the one and only time the pronoun 'he' is used. The rest of the time, the pictures convey hints about the way labour is gendered.

If asked about the gender of the duck before the end of the book, the temptation would be to name the duck as female. The duck is stooped, sleepy-eyed and deferential – and in the first spread, wearing an apron. But the duck does all the work of the farm, and in a brilliant sequence of six spreads the duck is shown doing both man's work and women's work: sawing wood, digging in the garden, washing the dishes, ironing, picking apples, and carrying eggs. A perfect sequence. The refrain is the same: "How goes the work?", says the farmer, and "Quack", answers the duck. The repetition brilliantly reinforces the tedium and repetitiveness of the tasks. At the end of the day the duck is shown as depressed: "sleepy and weepy and tired" – exactly the way most women feel after a day of underpaid, undervalued repetitive work.

Gender relations are played out as power relations. There is none of the heavy-handedness that typifies dogmatic attempts at redressing the inequities of our cultural inheritance. Instead, the gender issues are rendered (helpfully I think) in terms of patriarchal society, in terms of oppressors and oppressed. At the end of *Farmer Duck* all the animals work on 'their' farm. Here, too, there is a teasing question implied in the pictures. One of the students in an undergraduate class pointed out that even though everyone looks happy, it is the duck who is now ordering the others about. A hint of the oppressed becoming the oppressor? I don't know.

Books that suggest questions to be explored are the sort that will make a difference to our perceptions of gender difference. I'll leave the last word on the subject to Madeline Grumet, from *Bitter Milk*, her fine book on women and teaching:

> A curriculum designed for my child is a conversation that leaves space for her responses, that is transformed by her questions. It needn't replicate her language or mine, but must be made accessible to our interpretation and translation.

Conversation, interpretation, translation. They make the difference. The language of negotiation. Not gender wars.

LISSA PAUL

Great Adventures and
Everyday Events

SUE ADLER

Writing about Flournoy and Pinkney's well-known picture book, *The Patchwork Quilt*, a children's book specialist noted "There are no great adventures here, but the simple everyday events on which it focuses are endowed with depth and significance." (Hook, 1990)[1]. I have used this as a title and starting point for my brief investigation into gender and children's books, because that phrase 'great adventures' reverberated in my mind. I understand that the sense in which he is using the phrase is a widely accepted one – 'adventure' implies an exciting sequence of happenings, with conflict and, at the end of the story, resolution. Yet life, love, relationships – the themes in this children's story of family life – are, to me as a woman and feminist, great adventures in a deeper sense. The usual sense of this phrase, and my parallel interpretation of it, seem to identify a significant gender difference.

Authors and readers of fiction look inward to the emotions and outward to action. And while it is tempting tc polarise the two elements, categorising one as "going into the known and familiar" and the other as "going out into the unknown", I do not think these directions are mutually exclusive, or even that obvious. The 'known' in children's books - usually home life - can be full of excitement and imagination; the interplay of people can be of great interest and a dynamic source of tension. Exploring the 'unknown' with bold and fantastic voyages can be the flip side of fear, a symbolic way of transcending one's own smallness and powerlessness.

Dragon-slaying or, symbolically, conquering fear/evil – work for the strong and brave and occasionally canny – can be empowering for the reader who identifies with the adventurous hero (almost invariably male). But equally, it can be empowering to recognise and value non-symbolic portrayals of challenging and often confusing situations – such as the aging of Tanya's beloved grandmother in *The Patchwork Quilt*. Just as there are times when resolution is called for (the happy ending is a keynote in the conventional adventure plot and is necessary to give safety to the fantasy), there are times when an emphasis on continuity, and a recognition of the cycle of life and death, enable a child reader to experience a deeper kind of adventure.

The emphasis that authors choose to apportion to emotion and action, realism and fantasy, varies greatly. And, as an active participant, the reader, too, selects from the text to establish her or his own balance and personal interpretation. For example, in *A Difficult Day* by Eugenie Fernandes, the subject is realistic – a small girl sleeps badly, wakes up grumpy, is late for school, quarrels with her mother, sulks and finally hides under the bed. There is also a 'dream' sequence, where the child goes away –"to the other side of the world. The people there will love me and they'll hug me when I feel sad". While appreciating the imaginary scenes, the over-riding impact of the book lies, for me, in the relationship between the child and her mother. I do not find the domestic element in any way mundane – rather, the 'ordinariness' of the situation, highlighted and made special by being the subject of a book, gives the work interest and strength. In my own reading of this book, the 'adventure' lies not in the child's fantasy but in the human drama of being a child, the drama of insecurity and irritability and, of course, maternal love.

Reading as a woman or a girl may be quite different from the male experience. We – adults and children – necessarily read as individuals: gendered, of course. Sex, class, ethnicity, culture, life-experience, age, ideas, even mood, all shape our understandings and interpretations of texts. Reading is now recognised as a complex relationship between author, text, and reader, with the text no longer seen as having the same effect on each and every reader. What we understand and remember links the text to us – the interpretation is always subjective and is changeable. Readers – even very young, new readers – always bring themselves to the text. The words become meaningful because they stimulate a memory, provoke imagination, touch on an idea.

How children make sense of texts is an area both under-researched and difficult to research. The most recent and detailed study I know of examines racism and literature. Beverley Naidoo's *Through whose eyes?* documents white thirteen- and fourteen-year-old girls' and boys' responses to four novels. She notes instances where there are gender differences, commenting, for example, on girls' sense of conscience and their inclination to explore affective dimensions. Gender issues were not the focus of her research, yet she found it appropriate and significant – perhaps even inevitable - to consider them.

There seems to be a marked difference in the ways girls and boys read and understand texts, as well as in their reading preferences. However, in education, as elsewhere, the male experience is frequently the only one acknowledged and valued – the way in which Piaget equated boys' development with children's development in general is the obvious example of this. Much feminist work – including work on children's literature and reading – sets out to make visible female experiences, acknowledge difference, and appreciate female-defined values.

Research with adults provides insights that are relevant to teachers, librarians, and others with an interest in children as readers. Elizabeth Flynn and Patrocinio Schweickwart, in their introduction to *Gender and Reading: essays on readers, texts, and contexts*, give details of the responses of two (adult) students to William Faulkner's story *Spotted Horses*, demonstrating that gender is a huge factor in these responses. They observe that the male student is detached from the characters; he takes the stance of the critic-in-training. The female student "reacts emotionally as well as intellectually to the story".

The authors refer (as does Beverley Naidoo) to the influential work of Louise Rosenblatt (1978), and her belief that readers have different purposes for reading and read in different ways depending on those purposes. Rosenblatt distinguishes between 'aesthetic' reading, which involves experiencing the text fully, living through the events of the texts as they are encountered, and 'efferent' – from the Latin 'efferre' meaning to carry away – reading, which involves reading in order to take something away from the experience and make something of it[2]. On the whole, the former describes a feminine experience of reading, the latter a masculine one.

In the same volume, David Bleich documents the different ways that adults have of retelling stories. In his study, men told the facts, in a chain of information. Women presented the atmosphere, and were more likely to make inferences and respond affectively. Bleich writes, "Perhaps another way of articulating the difference would be that women enter the world of the novel, take it as something there for that purpose; men see the novel as a result of someone's action and construe its meaning or logic in those terms". (Flynn and Schweickwart, 1986) The researcher Carol Gilligan (1982) also discusses studies based on telling stories. She notes that the male responses to pictures and scenarios tended to focus on high adventure and violence. Women concerned themselves with establishing relationships and intimacy between characters. In each case, the same prompts were used, with very different results, and very different approaches to the construction of the story, and to adventure and danger.

If experienced 'story-tellers' and readers respond so differently, what about young girls and boys? I find the work of Carol Gilligan and Bronwyn Davies especially interesting and influential.

Gilligan's analysis of male and female difference, detailed in her book *In a Different Voice*, includes research on young children. In a chapter entitled 'Images of relationships', she documents the response of two eleven-year-olds to a moral problem. The boy, Jake, presents a clear solution to the problem, based on his mathematically defined view of logic. He uses the imagery of violence in his response, depicting a world of danger and hostile, explosive, confrontation. Amy, the girl, responds contextually rather than categorically. She is concerned with connections, saying "if you have a responsibility *with* somebody else, you should keep it". Amy sees a world of care and protection and life lived with others, whom "you may love as much or even more than you love yourself."

Gilligan traces a trajectory of development through the children's responses. "For Jake, development would entail coming to see the other as equal to the self and the discovery that equality provides a way of making connections safe. For Amy, development would follow the inclusion of herself in an expanding network of connections and the discovery that separation can be protective and need not entail isolation." These differences in ways of thinking about connection and separation are fascinating, and highly relevant to those working with children. It seems very likely that they enter into the way that children read, and shape their concepts of what count as 'great adventures'.

Bronwyn Davies is an educationalist and researcher who has studied children, their books, and the social construction of gender in depth, with a feminist perspective on the complexity and contradictions of the subject. In *Frogs and snails and feminist tales*, she takes a close look at young children's identification with characters, documenting responses of girls and boys to Robert Munsch's *The Paper Bag Princess*, a book she labels as 'feminist' (although I believe 'anti-sexist' is more appropriate). Indisputably an 'adventure' story, *The Paper Bag Princess* has a dragon (that fantasy beast so often used metaphorically), a princess, and a prince. It cleverly subverts fairytale conventions by portraying a brave, spirited princess and a pernickity prince.

I think these retellings that she quotes by two preschool children show a sharp and gender-related contrast:

ANIKA'S STORY

Princess Elizabeth loves Prince Ronald, but "he is just ignoring her, and she's putting all her love to him and that's wasting her love". The dragon burns the castle down and carries off Prince Ronald. Princess Elizabeth "feels angry". Elizabeth plans to make the dragon really tired by "making him do all the things lots of times". Ronald is a mean person so Elizabeth is "rude" to him. (Davies, 1989)

SEBASTIAN'S STORY

A prince and princess are about to get married. The dragon burns the castle and Ronald is high up in the air. Ronald very cleverly holds on to his tennis racquet tightly which is why he stays up in the air. Elizabeth and Ronald are both angry. The dragon goes home. Elizabeth "tricks the dragon because she wants to get her prince back". Prince Ronald tells Elizabeth to clean herself up "because he didn't like her being so messy". He is a nice person and she should clean herself, just as Sebastian has to do when he is dirty, no matter how hard it is to get the dirt off. It is all right that they don't marry each other because "he married someone else." (Davies, 1989)

Anika sees *The Paper Bag Princess* entirely as a story about relationships.

But love, the pivot of the story for her, has little place in Sebastian's version. He focuses on the plot, viewing Elizabeth only as a grubby, manipulative girl. The failure of the romance does not bother Sebastian, as a substitute wife quickly appears – in the boy's imagination, not in the text itself. He does not regard Elizabeth (as the author intended) as an admirable heroine. In fact, none of the children in Davies' study are particularly convinced by the anti-sexist messages of the text; they 'read' so subjectively that their own views are stronger than the adult author's. At five years old, their gender identity and knowledge of 'appropriate' female and male behaviour is highly conventional, and yet quite sophisticated. Impeccable anti-sexist tales – to our adult eyes – can be created to challenge sex-stereotypes. It's not so easy to convince the children!

But what is clear is that these two children have experienced the same book, enjoyed it – and interpreted it quite differently. That they have identified with their same-sex character in the book is one element; that they have read 'aesthetically' and 'efferently' another. The two versions show how, for one child, the adventure in the story, what keeps her turning the pages, relates to the feelings two characters have about each other. For the other child, the prince is the main character, it is his actions which make the story interesting.

These examples show how males and females may tell themselves different versions of the same story. Allied to this is the question of the books they choose in the first place – this is a difference that occurs before any reading and interpretation takes place. By now, there is little contention over the gendered differences of reading preferences. Kimberley Reynolds, in *Girls only? Gender and popular children's fiction in Britain, 1880-1910* explores issues surrounding 'girls' books' and 'boys' books', giving the subject a historical perspective. Drawing on the theories of Nancy Chodorow, Bruno Bettleheim, and Freud, she provides some explanations of gender differences in reading preferences and in understanding. She finds that girls and women, 'aesthetic' readers, tend to appreciate depictions of relationships, feelings, and fine details. Males tend to like facts, indicating that they are 'efferent' readers, and exciting adventure stories with lots of overt action and not too much introspection. They hardly ever choose anything to do with feelings. The subject of boys' reading has also been extensively documented in *Empire boys: adventure in a man's world*, a study which shows how masculine values, imperialism, and colonialism are related to one another. And while girls, as teachers know, are often prepared to read so-called 'boys' books', boys reject, at least publicly, 'feminine' books, often with a contempt that shows a frightening degree of misogyny and homophobia. Gender difference, then, can be seen in the initial choice of literature –

novel or spy thriller? 'Cosmopolitan' or 'Angling Times'? *A Difficult Day* or *Thomas the Tank Engine*? – or it can be evidenced, as I have been exploring in this article, in the aspects of the book that appeal to readers' imaginations and which they choose to dwell on. As I have tried to show, girls and women find within the text those elements that are interesting to them as girls and women. Often avid readers (including of a vast range of adventure stories), girls and women have the 'advantage' in a sexist society of being bicultural, of having, perhaps needing, to understand both the masculine and feminine worlds. Many girls do read 'masculine' adventure stories, empathising with the male characters and enjoying the thrill of the action; it would be a huge distortion to state that all girls always read for deep, emotional content only. But certainly, even in such reading, there is a trend towards finding the 'human' qualities of and connections in, of a story.

As I have written elsewhere (Adler, 1993), I think it is time in the debate on children's literature to re-evaluate the qualities we look for in texts, and to change our view of the significance of domestic, commonplace and everyday events, stories of mothers and daughters, and interpersonal relationships. We have simplified issues of gender and reading, sometimes seeming to suggest that all that was needed was to redress the gender balance, and provide stories in which girls were seen in 'strong' and 'active' roles. In doing so, we have devalued the importance of less obviously heroic kinds of fictions. The emphasis on 'ordinary lives' found in so many feminist books for adults (including novels, biographies, histories) can be, and sometimes is, an important focus for children's literature too. It will be real progress, perhaps even a great adventure, when we can explore these 'everyday events' in classrooms without 'boring' and antagonising boys – and without always having to face the chaos that results from trying to change the status quo a little. It will be real progress when all can acknowledge the value of books that do not romanticise unknown one-off happenings – as epitomised by Peter Pan's "Death must be an awfully big adventure" – but that do celebrate and value our lives and lived experience.

SUE ADLER

NOTES
1   John Hook in *Hooked on Books*. HBJ, 1990
His annotation is glowing and he recommended the book highly, commenting on its warmth and sensitivity. The noted lack of 'adventure' is clearly not meant as a derogatory criticism.

2   Louise Rosenblatt refers to the reader as 'he'. In a work published in 1978, this should, I think, be considered to be a historical use of the (false) generic.

A Traveller Family

PIP OSMONT

Through my work as a teacher for the Traveller Education Team, I met the Wards, an Irish traveller family. They had moved onto a piece of waste land in south east London to join relatives. The site was a dismal place, mostly tinned up, with the remains of earth banking all around the edges, put there to keep out unwelcome trespassers. The ground was rough, uneven, and muddy. There was no water supply although the council provided a skip and chemical toilets. This was a tolerated site.

Martin, the father, approached me about school places for his children. I asked him for their names and ages. Kathleen 12, Michael 11, Sabrina 10, James 9, Breda 8, Annie Rose 6. Later I found out about Martin 5, Chondelle 4, Joe 3, Sylvia 2 and Declan soon to be born. Had they been to school before?, I asked. Kathleen, Michael, Sabrina and James had been for a good few weeks back in Ireland. Could any of them read? No.

The nearest primary school couldn't provide places for all the children. The school that could was too far away for them to reach. I visited the family quite often while I was in the process of finding places. The children either ran away and hid from me, or stood and stared unresponsively when I spoke to them.

Eventually they started school, and, although they were given a warm welcome, they remained withdrawn and isolated. Looking back, they tell me how frightened they were, how the building was too big, with too many stairs, and how unkind some children were to them. After a while they seemed to settle, but their attendance was poor, and they made little obvious progress with reading. Sabrina, however, had a real talent for storytelling and, during the times that I spent with her in her class, she retold a story that she had listened to on the classroom tape-recorder. It was based on a fairy story and was about a poor girl (Brenda) who longed for a life where she didn't have to do so much housework. It had a happy ending! We made it into a book and Sabrina read this to me most times that I saw her.

Just before Christmas, the council evicted the families: the ground was needed to make a car park. They all moved on to another piece of waste land, and the search for school places began again. The parents would only consider the nearest school, which could offer just one place. It took three months to complete the appeal process.

On visiting the children in their new classrooms, I was surprised to find that Sabrina had become an independent reader. What was the reason for my surprise? Well, I had thought that there was much to prevent the children's progress. They had had little sustained schooling, there were few material resources and they lived in appalling conditions.

Not long after this revelation, I found out that Kathleen, then 13, and not in school, had also learnt to read. I became intrigued by how this had happened and started to ask tentative questions. Finding out took time, as the family tended to be very reserved with 'country people'. But gradually the girls opened up and it was then impossible not to listen to what the other children had to say as well.

My first question was how had they learnt to read? Sabrina explained that in the previous school she had learnt about letter sounds. She had also learnt to read a few words, and this had given her enough information to begin to make sense of the books that she occasionally brought home from school. Kathleen had joined in this endeavour and while Sabrina was not in school the girls had worked together on the task of reading the 'Sun' newspaper.

Why were they determined to read?

Martin, their father, had lived in a house and had been to school until he was fourteen. He regularly read the newspaper at home. Both girls had wanted to be able to do the same. Mary, their mother, had not been to school at all, because of travelling around, but had learnt the rudiments of the alphabet and had taught herself to read 'a little bit'. She had helped both girls as much as she could and Martin had helped with longer words.

The other children began to tell me about what motivated them. For Michael, it was his mother. She encouraged him to persevere even though he wasn't finding reading easy. For James, it had been a brief experience of school, back in Ireland, when he was seven. Just seeing the other children reading had made him want to do the same. Although Michael was struggling with reading, James perceived him as being a better reader than Sabrina. 'He knows 400 words, Sabrina knows 100'. The younger girls Breda and Annie Rose want to read like their older sisters. Martin and Chondelle were not forthcoming about their feelings.

My third question was whether they knew why they wanted to be able to read? There was no hesitation. The five oldest children all wanted to be able to read the newspaper. They also wanted to be able to read street and road signs. Apparently they have an uncle who can't read, and he keeps on getting lost. Shopping is a big consideration. Michael had recently been shamed by his mother, who told me that she had sent him out for shampoo but that he had come home with bubble bath. Breda said that if she didn't learn to read she "might buy the wrong things and you could die". Kathleen and Sabrina also mentioned wanting to read library books (originally learnt about from the T.V.). So did John. The girls laughed derisively at this news. Apparently John refuses to put in the necessary time at home, to the task of learning lists of words. This is the learning strategy that they all use, although the older girls complain that the younger ones don't remember what they have been taught. Both the girls and the boys said that they wanted to be able to read the words on the T.V. screen, and of course the T.V. guide in the newspaper.

Family relationships are close, and the girls and boys willingly help each other and share their knowledge. But it is evident that the girls are outstripping the boys in reading skills. There is, however, no marked difference in the girls' and boys' enthusiasm for reading. 'The Sun' newspaper, one much used 'World Wrestling Federation Magazine', the T.V., and occasional borrowed books are the reading sources in their trailer. How the girls and boys use them is quite different.

In the newspaper, Kathleen and Sabrina enjoy the problem page, the letters column, the human interest stories, the stars, the romantic comic-strip, and the T.V. guide. Apart from the T.V. guide this material is similar in context to fiction books. Michael and James choose differently. They like the simplest cartoon, the T.V. guide, the stars, the sport, and some pieces of news. Michael mentioned that the sports coverage in the 'Mirror' newspaper was better, as it included more on boxing, a sport that he participates in. He had, however, never read the 'Mirror'. Their sisters try to help them with this reading, although James is very resistant to being helped.

'The World Wrestling Federation Magazine' is popular with both the girls and the boys. Kathleen and Sabrina enjoy reading about these wrestlers, and are particularly intererested in the bits about their home lives. Michael and James are more interested in the abilities of these 'Super Heroes' They talked animatedly about the wrestlers' skills, and about who had beaten who. They knew so much, not because they could read the magazine, but because they watched this sport on T.V. The wrestlers looked similar to cartoon characters and Michael mentioned how much he liked cartoons. He said that he liked the reading scheme books at school because they had cartoon style illustrations. James also enjoys them.

When books (usually fiction) come into the trailer, Kathleen will read them to the children unable to read independently. James and his younger brother Martin refuse to join in. They both say "it is boring"; when they work with me in school both boys prefer to make fact books, James ones about boxing, and Martin ones which are simple picture and work books. Their sisters, on the other hand, make numerous story books, and even Chandelle includes a story alongside her pictures.

Michael and his cousin Tony (13) get together and play with their uncle's 'computer games'. They also enjoy looking at the catalogue that goes with these games. It is full of pictorial information in the form of episodes from the games. There are also very short written instructions.

Michael makes a great effort to read these to Tony.

Breda, Annie Rose, Martin, and Chondelle all say that they don't read at home and they they only read at school. Breda says that they had nothing to read at home, a remark which emphasises the importance of PACT schemes. She did add, however, that they read each other's writing.

In this family the newspaper has been a very valuable support to reading. Both girls and boys have been able to find material of enough interest to encourage them to persevere in this learning. Kathleen now visits the library, and also uses a dictionary to help her to understand more of the words she encounters. Michael, although making slow progress, still copies out lists of words from the newspaper to learn. Sabrina is busy at home writing her own stories, and Breda likes to learn words alongside Michael. The younger children are all eager to write and draw at home, and constantly ask for paper and pens.

Do schools offer the same range of support to girls and boys? Girls are usually well catered for in primary schools. Classrooms often have a good supply of fiction. But are the kinds of reading material that the boys in this family prefer always available? Perhaps Kathleen and Sabrina were able to use the knowledge gained at school because it was embedded in a context that they could relate to. Perhaps boys would benefit if they too encountered a context that they could more readily identify with.

The Ward boys are certainly as enthusiastic as their sisters about reading, but it seems more of a struggle for them. There are many other boys who have similar reading interests to Michael, James, and Martin. Boys who prefer fact books to fiction, who like cartoons, comic style books, T.V. books, and magazines, who are interested in sport and the trials of strength between Super Heroes. These could be incorporated into the reading environment of schools, and give these children added support in becoming successful readers.

There are many factors that make reading acquisition difficult for traveller children who do not live on official Council sites. Constant evictions and frequent changes of school, or even minimal schooling, all mean disruption to the learning process. In schools, the children often face prejudice and abuse. In spite of these difficulties, the Ward children, with strong parental support, the newspaper, a tolerated site, and the opportunity for sustained schooling, have become or are becoming readers.

Pip Osmont

TEACHERS

3

From a Different Perspective

MICHAEL ANNAN

Accomplished reading and writing skills are very often a prerequisite for the acquisition of status in society, in terms of jobs and the way others view us, and it is for this reason as much as any other that reading has such a high profile in education. The controversy surrounding the various methods by which children are taught to learn to read demonstrates how crucial people feel this area of the curriculum to be. Like other teachers, I have always devoted a good deal of time and energy to ensuring the children I teach develop good reading skills, certainly for some of the above reasons.

The teacher's role includes, but goes beyond, direct teaching. Teachers provide the contexts for reading in their class; these will include the texts provided, and the opportunities for reading and discussion. The teacher is also a model of a reader, and how the children see the teacher as a reader is obviously linked to race, gender, and class.

As a black male teacher in a primary school, I believe I have a different perspective on gender and race issues, since my experiences are not the same as those of the majority of my colleagues. In exploring the complex subject of gender and reading, I can only look at my personal experiences in the classroom situations I try to promote. I feel I inevitably have a greater insight into the difficulties black children may encounter, either because of the colour of their skin or their culture. Because of this I attempt to give a high profile to race issues. In practice this means, first and foremost, attempting to ensure children fulfil their potential by having consistently high expectations of them, as well as helping to develop positive self images and trying to tackle racist behaviour in a constructive way.

My own identity as a teacher is obviously influenced by my race and gender. I have brought these perspectives to being a primary teacher. Like many men, at school I was encouraged to focus on science and maths subjects, and, probably as a result, I tend in the classroom to provide a lot of activities related to science, maths, and technology. As I will discuss later, this also has implications in terms of the provision of non-fiction.

I came into teaching through working with the under fives. This, of course, is an unusual age range for men to work with. I feel there are interesting issues about how men take on the role of the primary teacher, particularly within the predominantly female culture of the primary school. When I was working with under fives, one of my co-workers was also a black man, and he was a valuable model for me. We talked about how the accepted way of approaching young children seemed to be different from ours. This showed itself in many ways – for instance, we were aware that our reactions to children who hurt themselves, or who were fighting, were less demonstrative than those of our female colleagues.

We discussed alternative ways of behaving with young children, and the effects on their education of living in a largely female world, where even key elements in good practice – home corners, a particular approach to display – seemed to reflect a predominantly female culture. We both felt that there were other possible alternatives to some accepted good practice, and that it was important to consider whether some aspects of this practice, were the only options, or whether they had simply never been questioned. We agreed that we needed to make our own way through the orthodoxy.

When I was training to be a teacher, there were very few men on the course and significantly fewer black men. I was conscious, especially as an infant teacher, that all my teaching practices were in classes with white women teachers. I learnt an enormous amount from these teachers, but there seemed to be certain ways of doing things which they had in common – such as their way of talking to children – which did not come naturally to me. Once I was with my own class, I realised that I had to do it my own way. There, and without a model, that was inevitably harder. It has taken me time to find my own way through, and part of this has been to do with the dilemmas and uncertainties connected with gender and race in teaching.

As I have already said, my teaching may sometimes focus more on maths, science, and technology. Often, it is not so much a matter of featuring these particular curriculum areas, but of placing a very practical emphasis upon them. In other areas of school life there are also differences in my approach. On playground duty, for example, I am more likely to be kicking a football or throwing a ball than holding hands with children, and I know that I have less interest in certain aspects of the children's background than some of my colleagues. It seems essential to me that there should be room for different perspectives within primary practice.

But, as a black teacher I am continually made conscious that most primary schools are predominantly white, and for that matter middle-class, institutions. As such, they may not be set up to cater for the needs of black staff. This shows in all sorts of ways, from the automatic assumptions that are made about staff social events, to the treatment that black staff may meet from non-teaching staff (I was once challenged by a schoolkeeper as soon as I entered the playground – even by being there I apparently constituted a threat). In staff rooms, there are generally two opposite tendencies, one of which is to ignore the fact of difference, while the other is to continually highlight it, by referring all equal opportunities issues to the black teacher. It has been my experience that there are advantages in working in schools where there are a number of other black teachers, though this is not to say that this one factor solves all the problems. The issues involved in being a black male primary teacher are complex, due to the racial bias found both in schools and education, and in society as a whole, but I believe they are worthy of some serious thought and debate.

As a result of at least some of the factors discussed above, my approach to teaching literacy has always incorporated equality issues. At its most basic, this has meant attempting to ensure that all children get equal access to resources and support, while monitoring their progress to try and ensure all fulfil their potential. My view is that, since there are certain groups (in society in general and in school in particular) who, because of gender, race, class or disability, are disadvantaged, teachers need to address this imbalance with practical steps.

As far as girls' reading is concerned, there are obvious practical things to be worked on. In my experience, many girls between ages seven and eight years are well on the way to becoming accomplished readers, and they often have a positive attitude towards books and other types of print. However, as I observe them in the classroom, it is my perception that they do tend to select mainly story books; those studies which indicate that girls are less likely to read non-fiction seem accurate.

Frances is a confident reader, who is able to successfully tackle nearly all of the texts available in the reading area. She invariably chooses fiction books to read. During the third term of her year in my class, she began to complain about the lack of new books on the shelves. When I suggested she might try some of the non-fiction available, specifically books on the topic-focus table, Frances seemed reluctant, and needed quite a lot of encouragement before selecting this type of book to take home.

Jane is a similarly able reader, with a very positive attitude towards reading. When I came to examine a list of books that she had selected to take home over the first two terms, they proved to be nearly all fiction. She responded well to my suggestions to take some non-fiction books home, but it was quite obvious that, without some intervention, her initial choice would probably have been a story.

Ray, on the other hand, though an equally accomplished reader, spends a good deal of time reading non-fiction. He showed a particular interest in a set of atlases recently introduced into the class and would often sit with a group of others, predominantly boys, reading through them and discussing the position of particular countries, and who came from where.

For the particular group of girls I am concerned about above, it would not be enough simply to focus on the development of reading skills. Just as important is the type of reading material that they need to be more familiar with: factual books and print. If they remain detached from this kind of reading, they may not learn to read them as well as they read their preferred fiction books. Yet the ability to effectively extract information from such sources may be essential to them later in life, as well as later in their schooling.

Children's attitudes to reading, their view of themselves as readers, and their view of the adult readers they may become, are key factors in their reading development. We know that in terms of educational achievement, boys are not doing as well as girls. We are also aware of the underperformance of African-Caribbean boys as a group. Yet schools seem slow to address these known areas of underachievement.

I do not want to conjecture about reasons or answers to these issues until more subtantial work has been done to enquire into them. But I was interested to note, when considering successful readers in my class, that the black girls' racial and gender identity seemed to be more easily accepted within the school setting. In terms of equal opportunities, girls and their learning of maths and science are now on everybody's agenda. Perhaps it is time to put issues of race, gender, and boys' reading on the agenda?

Like most teachers, I consider reading to be central to all learning that takes place in the classroom, and have spent time carefully considering the implications of the issues I have been discussing, and trying out various strategies. The practical classroom provision I make for reading has two main strands to it: firstly the resources – the range of reading material available – and secondly the adult support that children get in tackling this material.

Given that different children's experiences of reading outside school can be very wide-ranging, I try to provide a selection of reading material that attempts to reflect, and therefore indirectly acknowledge, all these experiences. All children should be able to come into my classroom and find reading material that they are familiar and confident with. This will include fiction and non-fiction, dual language texts, magazines, comics, newspapers, catalogues, telephone directories, 'home-made' books, maps and atlases, and any other suitable form of print. I aim to create an environment in which it is possible to build on and widen the experiences of all, thus making success in reading more likely for everyone and not just a select few.

Next, it is necessary to consider the actual content of the print provided. Although the 'Sun' newspaper may be in a number of homes, it would, for obvious reasons, be completely unsuitable to to have copies available in school. I want all the children to meet images of people that they can relate to, and see those people in a generally positive light, taking a real part in society. If they cannot find themselves in the books they read in school, they may feel left out of the world of print.

We are more used now to looking at the way in which, in all media, versions of the world are promoted that affect the way we see both others and ourselves. The gross gender stereotyping that used to be found in school reading books is something that we are much more conscious of now. We know that this stereotyping works against both girls and boys – both need to encounter stories where female characters can occupy central roles, and act decisively and with authority. Both need to meet male characters in non-traditional roles – and in roles where their capacity to reveal their feelings and to look after others can be expressed.

For black children, there will be a particular importance about the way in which the books in their classroom and in the school as a whole show black characters – and whether they show them at all. Outside of school, white children have a mass of positive images to relate to in all forms of media, but even today this is not true for black children. It is only in school that we can go some way towards redressing the balance and providing these different kinds of images and experiences. If children consistently see people whom they can relate to in a positive light, they are much more likely to feel good about themselves and feel part of the world of the school, and they have a greater chance of fulfilling their potential.

There is now a growing selection of fiction and non-fiction texts that are written from new perspectives and reflect a wider range of experience. Books like *Jamaica Tag-along, Little Monster, Marcellus, Bet You Can't, Grampa's Face, Mom Can Fix It,* and others allow black and white children the opportunity to see black people and women/girls in key roles, and can also be used by teachers to help children become aware of stereotyping. It's not enough simply to provide the images and hope that these issues will be resolved by themselves. Books need to be shared and discussed. The whole process of becoming a critical reader, of examining the assumptions behind texts and the standpoints of authors, is involved in this questioning of the traditional roles given to women, men, and black people in books.

Having provided resources that both reflect more of the children's experiences and are anti-racist and non-sexist, my main concern is obviously how best to use them in supporting children's learning. Equal opportunities issues sometimes risk being seen as separate from the mainstream, so I attempt to ensure that the resources described are an integral part of the daily reading routine. This routine includes individual, shared and silent reading. I also try to allow choice in terms of reading partners, what children read, and where they read, so the sessions are relaxed, and children feel self-motivated.

Though there are no strict patterns with regard to who reads with whom, there is a group of boys and girls, approximately six of each, who invariably read with another child of the same sex. The other children in the class seem quite flexible about who they read with, though the content of the book appears to influence their choice. As I mentioned earlier, Ray tends to sit and share a set of atlases with a group mainly consisting of boys. There are books like *Jamaica Maddah Goose* which, at least initially, appeal to certain groups of children.

I have found paired reading to be especially effective in building the confidence of individuals, and it gives them a chance to tackle more taxing texts than might otherwise be possible. It also readily lends itself to small group discussion about the content of the material being read and how it relates to the readers. When I listen to individuals or pairs of children reading texts, either those they have chosen themselves or those which we have selected together, there is an opportunity to discuss the characters and storyline.

When Carla came to the part in the *Piggybook* where Mr Piggott and sons search the floor for food, she commented that they were nasty and seemed very disgusted with their behaviour. She said she felt they should have kept the place clean and cooked food for themselves. Then with Nadine, whom she was sharing the book with, we discussed whether Mrs. Piggott should return and then who did the washing, ironing, etc. in their own homes.

Central to my approach is the use of the *Primary Learning Record*, which allows me to regularly identify individuals' strengths and weaknesses, and then decide upon support children need. It is also very useful in monitoring the progress of groups of children who historically have failed to gain equality of opportunity. The observation sheets included in the *Learning Record* emphasise reading across the curriculum, and so encourage an awareness of children's experiences with print other than those in the reading area. One fundamental principle in a reading curriculum should obviously be to try and introduce some form of reading in all areas of the curriculum.

As part of any topic, I make a point of getting children to help select reading material from libraries, either the school or the local library, that is relevant to the work we will be doing. In the summer term, at the beginning of a topic on life and living things, I asked a group of children, accompanied by a primary helper, to go to the school library and select books relevant to the topic. The group came back and introduced the texts they had chosen to the whole class, at which time we considered how we might use them, and, sometimes, whether or not they were appropriate. Then the books were displayed and formed a focus for the topic, along with artefacts that could be referred to.

When reading is included in tasks that are related to all areas of the curriculum, children gain more experience of a wider range of texts, and are also given the opportunity to seek for information from print for a real purpose. In at least in some cases, they will not otherwise have had the chance to read this kind of material. A number of computer programmes aimed especially at year three and onwards e.g. *Pip goes to the moon, Nature Park Adventures, Yellow Brick Road, Through the Dragon's Eyes,* and *Space Mission Mada,* also lend themselves to this kind of functional reading, and girls must have easy and frequent access to them.

I believe it is possible, through books, print and a variety of other media, to help children to recognise and then acknowledge their identities, and sometimes their origins. This will be particularly important for children whose communities or countries of origin are traditionally viewed in a negative way. For instance, the views of Africa and Africans that children generally meet are often damaging, and degrading. Stories like *Bimwilli and the Zimwi, Oh Kojo* and a selection of newer non-fiction can prove useful in beginning to counteract the view of Africa often found in the media. Again, just leaving these books about or occasionally reading them aloud will not accomplish much. If children are to begin to make links between the books and their lives, it will be necessary to draw their attention to the characters and images in these texts and how they differ from others they may have met.

As black people, we are regularly exposed to racism in many forms. Having a strong sense of self-worth and belonging are vital in constructively combating this. My own experience has been that a heightened awareness and understanding of the culture and people of my country of origin has been a very positive influence on my life. I know, for example, how much I gain from regular trips to Ghana, in terms of feelings of belonging and pride in the ways and traditions of Ghanians in particular, and Africans in general.

My aim has been to approach issues of gender, race, and more generally equal opportunities by developing practice that at every step and in every aspect gives these issues a high profile, and ensures that children have access to the support and resources their different needs require. Then, by always attempting to be aware that, even given such a framework, there is a need for constant intervention, I hope to help all children fulfil their full potential. Without this, the other issues discussed relating to equality are meaningless.

MICHAEL ANNAN

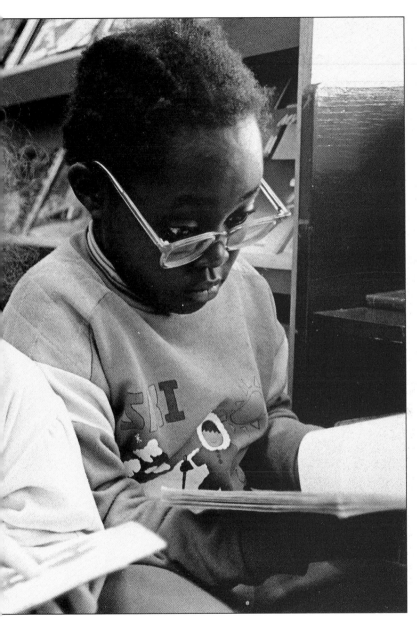

Sexing the Avocado Baby

SARA HAYNES

"She should get some better clothes and look nice", said Shazma, as if to conclude our discussion following *The Paper Bag Princess* at story time. This response is no longer one which surprises me, but it never fails to disappoint me. Similar comments have been made every time I have read this book with young children. This was not the first time these six and seven year olds had heard the story, or that we had talked about it, but I was struck again by the ambiguity of their response and the angle of their reasoning.

This time, at the end of the story, one child's immediate criticism of Elizabeth's "dirty and messy" appearance had led to a discussion of the clever and admirable things she had done. There was some consensus here: Elizabeth was acknowledged to be 'kind', 'brave', 'friendly', 'clever', and 'strong'. It was also agreed that Ronald was "not very nice to her at the end" and that "he should at least say thank you". Elizabeth's qualities are undoubtedly ones the children recognised and valued. However, as soon as we returned to the ending, the feelings about her clothes and her hair resurfaced, took over, and again became the focus for their comments. Shazma's idea was, I think, a move forward. She responded to the negative reactions with a possible resolution: Elizabeth could redeem herself by improving her appearance. Her bravery, loyalty and strength were in no doubt, but she was flawed; princesses in fairy tales should be perfect, and the prerequisite of perfection in a fairy tale princess is beauty.

This discussion reminded me of a previous conversation about princesses with two seven-year-old girls. *The Tough Princess* had elicited a positive response from Cathy: "She's not gentle and kind...yes I like this one. Princesses don't usually fight!" Later she began to describe a book that was a retelling of *Snow White and Rose Red*:

Sara: What's it about?
Cathy: Um, these two girls. I'll show you the pictures, There was this lady with two daughters (pause). Anyway they were sitting and weaving and stuff (pause). Eeugh! Not very pretty, are they Amy?
Anne: No!
Sara: Aren't they?
Anne: No! They're meant to be quite pretty.
Sara: Why do they need to be pretty?
Cathy: Because the prince marries them.

After reading the story we continued to talk:

Sara: Why do they need to be pretty to get married to the prince?

Cathy:	Because they have to be if (pause). He wouldn't marry them otherwise.
Sara:	Don't princes marry people who aren't pretty?
Cathy:	No.
Sara:	Well, what would make them pretty? (pause) What is pretty?
Anne:	Don't you know what pretty is?
Sara:	Well, do you think everyone thinks pretty is the same thing? I think those girls (in the picture) are quite pretty.
Anne:	No *they're* not pretty, *they're* horrible.
Sara:	Why are they horrible?
Anne:	They just are. They've got horrible things on and (pause).
Sara:	If you were drawing the pictures what would they look like?
Anne:	Well, they'd have white dresses on. No. Snow White would have a white dress on; Rose Red would have a red dress on, a light red one, and they'd have flowers and patterns on, and, um, it would (pause) and they would have a petticoat underneath 'cos, um, it's all made out of lace with lots of layers.

Girls, in particular, respond to the brave and thinking *Tough Princess*, and enjoy the power she has, but the visual impact of her appearance overrides her appeal. In order to understand the intentions and implications of fairy-tale reworkings with a feminist slant, children need to have a good knowledge of traditional tales. The message – and often the humour – of these stories depends on challenging expectations within an existing narrative structure, cast of characters and language conventions ('They biffed happily ever after'). Young children have often not read widely enough to appreciate this fully.

They also need a firmly established sense of their own gender-identity and their possibilities within it. To many children of this age, dressing in a way which announces their gender unequivocally, even stereotypically, is of great importance: relating to the heroines who challenge the importance of appearance in determining gender is difficult until they feel more definite about their own identity. At the same time, perhaps these books play a part in enabling children to see that, while their gender is important to them, it can be expressed in ways which are not as clear-cut as they may have thought, and that it does not need to limit them.

I find young children's growing awareness of challenges to stereotypes encouraging, but it struggles with, and is almost always superseded by, traditional assumptions and expectations. In Jill Murphy's *Whatever Next!*, Baby Bear is not identified as male or female for several pages. At the beginning of the story Khalid made a comment referring to the bear as 'she'. His assumption was actually, I think, that the bear was *male*, his confusion of pronouns common for a child new to English. Other children picked up on this 'mistake', and I pointed out that we had no clues so far to Baby Bear's gender. Hafsana commented that Baby Bear is wearing 'jeans' (dungarees) and a consensus was reached: he must be male. In the class that day, three girls were wearing jeans, and so was I. We all stood up. A further agreement was reached: we were all girls; we were all wearing jeans. We returned to the illustrations in the book, and Shazma (wearing jeans!) stated that "only boys wear jeans". Roqib seemed to recognise an inconsistency here, so introduced new 'evidence': "He's brave. Girls not go rocket!" The response to this was a claim to bravery from Halima, and murmurs of agreement from several other girls. As Roqib's 'evidence' was inconclusive, we reverted to a frustrating focus on the bear's clothes, and the finality of Pharvez's comment: "He wears jeans. He's a boy". Despite challenges, ultimately the image of Baby Bear was male for them. This is in line with their expectations and previous experience: animals in the books they know – *Spot, The Hungry Caterpillar, The Fat Ca*t, all the animals in *Dear Zoo* – are *male*. Of course, by page four, it is clear that Baby Bear is a boy.

Incidentally, it seems to me that Shazma's self-contradiction may express an unarticulated awareness that there *are* conventional representations of boys and girls in books, in magazines, and on T.V., and that these do not necessarily relate to real life. Knowing these conventions, it's possible that Shazma thought that a character in jeans was something she was *supposed* to recognise as a boy. (If the kitchen in the Fairy Liquid advent: looked anything like mine, the viewers would be appalled, yet we all accept the convention of the perfect T.V. kitchen, which has little relation to our own.)

Buying and making books with explicitly female animals in them goes a little way towards challenging assumptions about the gender of animal characters. Susanna Gretz's *Frog in the Middle* has two female animal characters and one male. We discussed it after the first reading, when it was a new book to the class. Halima speaks and reads English fluently. Her "How do you know it (Frog) is a girl, Sara?" demonstrates the strength of the general assumption that animals in books are male. When we looked through the text, we found that Frog was referred to as 'she' throughout.

These assumptions also apply to human gender. John Burningham's *Avocado Baby* is always referred to as 'it' in the book. A class of five and six year olds referred to the baby as 'he'. When challenged, their defence was that the baby had short hair, wore blue, had a 'boy's face', and was strong. It was quickly agreed that all babies have short hair and that a lot of girls in the class were wearing blue. Six of the eight girls present also said they were strong. At the end of the discussion, everyone, with the exception of one girl, still believed the baby was a boy. The next day Khadija and Rashida undertook a (teacher initiated) survey to find out if the adults in the school thought Avocado Baby was a girl or a boy. As she asked me the question, "Do you think Avocado Baby is a girl or a boy?", Rashida bent down conspiratorially and said, "But it is a boy". The survey showed that most adults in the school, given by the children the simple choice between boy and girl (and the opportunity to challenge the assumptions that the survey was testing!), thought that Avocado Baby was a girl. But the children were still not convinced. They agreed that there were no gender definitions in the text and were obviously searching for new evidence. Everyone seemed relieved when Shanaz pointed to the page, with the burglars and said excitedly, "I know! I know! If it's a girl, the baby will be scared".

The undercurrent of expectation that girls in books are less powerful than boys in books reflects – and is reflected by – boys' and girls' relative perceptions of themselves as readers. The pattern of reading fluency within our classes of six and seven year olds is typical: one boy and one girl who are exceptionally fluent readers; a large group of girls who are fluent readers progressing well; and a number of children who are at an early stage and who are predominantly boys.

I talked to the fluent readers about their reading. The moderately fluent boys considered themselves good readers. The girls who were more fluent underestimated their achievements. Khaleda claimed that she was not good at reading "cos I can't read all the books". Faridaha said that she was not good at reading, then modified this by saying she had got better recently.

Despite the girls' obvious enjoyment of reading, their perceptions of why they were learning to read were without exception pragmatic and functional, as extracts from some of their *Primary Learning Record* reading conferences show:

Faridah's dad reads Bengali newspapers; her mum doesn't read because she's cooking... Fulshana says you need to be able to read in the juniors and when you're grown up "to learn."

Khaleda can read some Bengali and she wants to learn some more so she can write to people in Bangladesh "like my Nan; she doesn't know English."
She says it was difficult to learn to read and you have to work hard at it.
"It's important to learn to read, because it helps you learn English, and if you go for interviews when you grow up you must speak English to get a job.

That's what happened to my Auntie cos she doesn't speak English." Halima's glad she has learnt to read because it will help her get a job and a big house and garden.

These girls demand a lot of themselves. Their achievements are never quite enough: they consistently intend to go further. Boys whose literacy skills are not as developed seem to be more easily satisfied with their achievements, and have greater self-esteem in reading.

The perception of learning to read as 'difficult', is, perhaps, not surprising in children belonging to a community where adult literacy is not taken for granted. Because they are determined that their children will achieve, many parents impress upon them the need to 'work hard' and 'do well'. Where no-one in the family can give specific help with reading, support is provided in other ways. One child described the family's response to her younger brother's first independent attempt at an English text: "Everybody one day gave him a clap, because he can read *Peace At Last*".

Bilingual girls in my class usually have few models of female readers at home: often their mothers, aunts, grandmothers, have had no opportunity for education. Reading must sometimes appear a skill that is difficult to acquire, even out of reach. Their mothers may not read at all; the girls' aim is to read in two or three languages. From all of this comes their perception that learning to read requires large amounts of work and commitment, that it will not come easily, even when they are achieving highly. This makes them less likely even than monolingual girls to believe that their efforts are being rewarded and that they are 'doing well'.

Where the children in my class *do* see adults reading at home, it tends to be men reading for *information* (or for religious purposes). When she saw a newspaper in a teacher's bag, Hafsna exclaimed that the (female) teacher must be a man. When we all admitted to reading newspapers, she insisted that "only men read newspapers", which was echoed by several other children.

This idea is reflected to some degree in the children's reading choices. It is well known that girls read more fiction than boys, and boys more non-fiction than girls. As I observe the choices at reading time and when children select books to take home, the difference is marked. Despite efforts to provide information books that appeal to girls and fiction that appeals to boys, girls predominantly choose fairy tales and legends and boys, while they do select favourite picture books, read more reference books.

Girls appear, from their comments in reading conferences, to think of learning to read as the acquisition of a practical skill to be used in a purely functional way. Nevertheless, in apparent contradiction to this, they do not choose to read information texts. At the risk of generalising, the internalised female cultural push towards fantasy and romance runs counter to their recognition that access to education and work depends on skills associated with reading, writing and interpreting fact. I have noticed that this dichotomy is perhaps particularly pronounced for these girls, who are part of a newly-established Asian community. In common with all girls, but perhaps to an even greater degree, they witness and experience a cultural expectation that girls and women will be fulfilled through their emotions, relationships, and families, the flip-side of which is housework and confinement to the home. Their choice of fiction is, in part, an acceptance of that expectation: reading fairy tales provides a way to explore the fulfilment 'second-hand' and to escape the flip-side.

But at the same time as the girls are exploring, through their reading of fiction, traditional 'feminine' preoccupations, (which reinforce their experience of traditional female roles at home), they are also being encouraged to work hard at school to prepare themselves for an active role *outside* the home. The implications of this contradiction, particularly pronounced in an Asian community, have not, I think, been fully recognised by the children, their families, or by their teachers.

Girls' earlier attainment of the fundamental skills in reading has implications for their success in other curriculum areas. In the classroom, girls are more likely to *choose* to work at reading and writing. Obviously they are learning these skills by using them more, but at what cost? While writing records this year, I noticed that the girls who are particularly fluent readers and writers are far less confident - and competent - in maths, science, and technology. Boys who are gaining reading fluency, though less quickly, have a greater balance in their achievement across the curriculum. (We are constantly working to balance boys' inclination to learn skills that will empower them in the outside world with girls' inclination to develop their abilities to express their inner selves.)

Other differences in the power attributed to different kinds of reading are highlighted for children who are learning to read in two or more languages. Even when attempts are made to provide books in other languages, and to reflect language diversity, English is the language of the curriculum and the language of most of the teachers. Many of the children state "learning English" as a primary reason for coming to school; most of the parents regard literacy in English as the children's access to success. Encouraging literacy in the home language is perceived as a way of maintaining family and cultural connections, while literacy in English is considered as a door to the exterior world of jobs.

The children believe that learning to read English is easier than learning to read in their home language. Halima explains this to me:

English is easier because when you learn Arabic and Bengali you have to wait one year to learn the alphabet and wait till all the children know it and then do the next bit.

Rabib said that he reads "sometimes Bengali but mostly English", and that it had been easier to learn to learn to read English "because when I was about five, I saw my brother and sister reading and I said 'I want to read, I want to read!' and my mum got picture books, and I learnt it in three days".

In our school, we have decided that offering a *choice* of reading material, within a teacher-selected range of books, is critically important in the acquisition of literacy. This makes maintaining a balance – between, for example, a girl's fiction and non-fiction reading – a challenge. Finding information books which appeal to girls is difficult, but not impossible: Shopna, who read only fiction, was introduced by a teacher to a book on hopscotch, one of the girls' favourite games. The book has since become very popular within her circle of (female) friends. We work towards increasing the number of books in the classroom that challenge gender stereotyping and assumptions, and those which encourage girls and boys to break traditional reading patterns.

Most children in the school, and particularly the girls, are, then, facing a range of challenges surrounding the – already considerable – challenge of learning to read. At the same time, they benefit considerably from parental support in their learning, in both mainstream and community language schools. Most of the children are as determined as their parents that they will read and write in English and their home language. The success of the girls in achieving this, given the relative lack of models of female readers within their own families, underlines their determination and application.

SARA HAYNES

(Thanks to Andrew Read for recording the *Avocado Baby* discussion, and to Kate Wilson)

Changing the Pattern

SUE ELLIS

As teachers, we are becoming increasingly aware of gender as an issue in children's development as readers. There is evidence in a growing number of studies, reports, and surveys (Julia Hodgeon, 1984, Pip Osmont 1987, ILEA Research and Statistics, 1986/1988/1990, Lewisham Survey, 1991, HMI 1990, *Testing 7 year-olds in 1991,* DES) which shows gender to be a significant factor affecting reading achievement and reading choice for boys and girls. Some general, rather broadly drawn conclusions reveal that, for example, boys are consistently over-represented in underachieving groups when compared with girls as readers, show marked preferences for non-fiction, and appear less interested in reading as they move through the primary school.

Often this evidence confirms the observations that teachers make in classrooms, though the detail of teacher observations also more clearly reveals the complexity of the issue. We recognise, for example, that there are a considerable number of children who don't fit these generalisations, and this alerts us to the danger of further stereotyping and the narrowing of expectations. However, the growing body of evidence from our own classrooms, combined with wider research, confronts us with patterns of difference that cannot be ignored. It helps to throw into sharp relief the need for us to work out ways of providing reading experiences which are responsive to the learning styles and interests of individuals. We need to explore ways of including and extending both boys and girls as readers, within and beyond the classroom.

Messages about what reading is for, and whom it's for, are powerfully communicated in schools, homes, and communities, and in society generally. From these messages, children construct a view of themselves as readers: what kind of reader, how successful they are, and what reading offers them, or doesn't. Schools and teachers, although not the only influence, can nevertheless make a significant impact on how individuals see themselves and how they develop as readers.

This chapter looks at some of the ways teachers work to create an inclusive reading environment. It has often been difficult, in thinking about these classrooms, to draw out teaching strategies and approaches that are specifically supportive in addressing issues of gender, because they are so embedded in good practice. The practice described here grows from a recognition of gender as an important factor in the education of children as readers, and an awareness of the need to take full account of each child's individual view of themselves as a reader.

Jill Verde and Alex Law are two teachers who take gender into account in considering the reading contexts and provision available in their classrooms. It is one focus among many that they use in reflecting on their role in promoting and supporting reading, and in observing children's development as readers. In this article, I shall describe some of the elements of their practice, and look at features that their classrooms have in common.

Reading aloud is a powerful way of helping to establish a community of readers in the classroom through the shared enjoyment and understanding of books and texts. Jill Verde, a teacher working with nine and ten year olds at Bannockburn School in Plumstead, strongly believes in the role of reading aloud as a central means of involving children in reading and books. Her practice of reading aloud, at least three times a day, a selection of familiar, less familiar, and unknown texts, enables her to access a wide range of material, which appeals to the spread of individual, as well as common, interests in the class. She links this to issues of gender:

> When I first began to think about boys' underachievement and waning interest in reading as they got older, I decided to choose class texts which tended to appeal more specifically to 'boys' interests'. I read aloud lots of action-packed stories and football yarns, which I was sure they would enjoy. I tried it for a while but realised that they actually only appealed to a small minority of the class, and then only for a limited time. What was really needed was the chance to hear a variety of authors and titles, so that there was something for everyone. I also felt that it was important not to underestimate what the children would be interested in. By frequently reading aloud I'm trying to extend the range of reading all the children do, by exciting them about all kinds of books, different authors and illustrators, or by getting them hooked on poetry, for example.

As children get older, many of the texts they read tend to be longer, and the practice of reading whole stories in serialised form needs to be expanded, if variety is to be sustained. This means that the selection of texts to read aloud might, in addition to serialised novels, include introductory chapters or particularly exciting episodes, individual poems, jokes and riddles, anthologies, picture books, favourite requests, newspaper and magazine articles, extracts from information books, notices about local events and exhibitions, and children's own writing. In Jill's classroom, children regularly read their favourite pieces aloud to the group, as well as their own writing. This creates opportunities for the children to swap books, and to broaden their interests through the powerful recommendations of peers.

Alex Law, who teaches a vertically grouped, upper junior class of predominantly bilingual childen in Sir William Burroughs School in Tower Hamlets, also gives priority to reading aloud.

> By reading to them, I help to make familiar the range of reading material in the classroom, and perhaps reduce some of the risk and disappointment there can be in choosing unknown texts or texts with unfamiliar tunes,

such as non-narrative forms. We deliberately spend time reading informa-tion texts aloud, so that the children have some experience of how they sound and how they can be read. If it's important to read aloud stories and poetry, then it must be worthwhile to do the same with information books. Often, the children find they enjoy stories, information books, and authors they might not have selected to read for themselves. It opens up different possibilities. The chance to talk about books together during this time is really important for developing their interest and understanding, and for giving me an idea of the books that work well. Treating reading as a social, as well as an individual, activity is supportive and seems to make it all the more enjoyable. The impact is really clear in their reading diaries. What I read to them is very influential in what they then choose to read by themselves, for both boys and girls.

Alex is also aware of the predominance of female readers in most chil-dren's lives at home and school. She values team-teaching with her col-league Graham, who can provide boys with a positive model of an adult male reader, and is concerned to ensure that other male readers (teach-ers, parents, members of the community) are regularly invited to read aloud or to tell stories to the class. Tape recordings of stories, plays, poems, and appropriate information texts read by male as well as female voices are provided (drawing on parents, teachers, boys, radio broadcasts as well as published versions), as another way of helping to redress the balance. Many of these are recorded in the range of languages spoken by the children.

The provision of books and materials is obviously a crucial factor in ensuring that all children's needs and interests are catered for. Alex is aware of the need to offer sufficient range to provide new and different challenges to readers of all levels of experience. Getting the balance right is a continuous process of updating and building a collection of books, tapes, videos, and software based on what the teacher knows works well, the range of writers and genres the children need to encounter, and the preferences and interests expressed by individuals through child confer-ences, reading journals, home-school diaries, and conversations with chil-dren and parents. She feels it is important to build on children's interests from home in order to extend their reading.

Many of the boys in my class are really keen on comics. We keep a selec-tion in the book area and this recognises and validates their interest in the school setting. They are a powerful influence on the boys' writing, which you can see from the books they've made. I've also built up a col-lection of fiction and information books in cartoon format, which are popular with boys and girls, particularly bilingual girls. I do make sure that they read other material as well, by varying the focus of quiet read-ing times, making the comics available on certain days only, and recom-mending books I think individuals will enjoy.

Alex responds to the interest expressed in animal books by many of the girls in her class by ensuring that a range of books are available on the subject.

> This includes stories about animals as well as a range of information books, from *Eyewitness Guides* to 'Big Books' to newspaper articles and children's own accounts. The children also know when I'm going to the Schools' Library Service, and will often ask me for particular books and authors, or for the kinds of books they want. It's important that children develop their own tastes and preferences as readers. It's a sign of a committed reader, and that's a useful place to build from. Whilst respecting and encouraging their interests, as a teacher you're always trying to show them what else there is.

In reviewing the range of reading material available in her classroom, Jill has been steadily increasing the number of information books with a strong narrative style:

> For most children, most readers, narrative is a more accessible form, and publishers are beginning to realise there is a demand for information books written in a more user-friendly style, like David Macauley's books for example. It's a useful way of building bridges for children, particularly girls who may not gravitate towards information texts as readily as some boys. That's not to say we don't work with more conventional information books; children need to feel confident in using those too. But they need a variety of ways in.

Having a good range of books and materials in the classroom is a beginning, but it's essential to provide effective classroom routines to ensure all children have real access to the texts on offer. The use made of regular reading times in the classroom is an aspect of reading provision Alex has re-examined after noticing that some children, many of them boys, seemed not to settle to read in a sustained way, or appeared to read from a very limited range of material.

> I decided to vary the nature of quiet reading times, to provide more rigour and focus to the sessions. We'd fallen into a routine, which had ceased to be effective for all the children. The pattern of Graham, (my team teacher partner), and I reading our own books whilst the children read theirs was extended to include working with small groups of children for shared reading with big books, rotating boxes of books containing specific genres so that children would meet a broader range of texts, planning the use of the tape-story area and the computer so that all children had access to them, and having paired reading and individual reading times. We also decided to spend some of this time with individual readers, particularly those who needed more support, talking about choosing books, their preferences, and who they liked reading with, as well as reading together. We'll often come together afterwards as a whole group, to

share favourite pieces and recommend titles. The children are also encouraged to say if they didn't enjoy or understand a book, and to try to explain why. If they are going to develop as mature readers, they need to become critical, discriminating readers. I find it useful to know what they really think, from the point of view of ordering books which will appeal.

Jill Verde tends to use quiet reading times as an opportunity to observe children's individual reading patterns and preferences.

> I can see what children choose to read, and who they choose to read with. I watch how they go about choosing books. I also notice if they seem to be reading the same kind of text time and time again. Often, of course, that's perfectly valid, revisiting texts is important, but it helps me to see where children are stuck and judge when I need to intervene.

Being aware of children's individual reading needs and interests is crucial for appropriate, effective support to be offerred. Jill uses a variety of ways of getting to know her children as readers.

> The *Primary Language Record* reading conferences are a very useful way of finding out about the children as readers, and by that I mean talking with parents as well as children. I've found some of the information a real revelation, for example children who write plays at home or are real gardening experts, which I wasn't aware of but can build on in the classroom. With others I've managed to gain insights into their difficulties with reading, and have used conferences to begin establishing a sense of trust and confidence. But conferences aren't enough on their own. We regularly write journals, where children record their comments about the books they read. Home-school reading diaries are another means of keeping in touch with what children are reading. And, of course, there are the classroom observations I make, too.

Alex, too, values collecting evidence of her children as readers in a variety of ways, so that she can offer them the best support possible. She uses the *Primary Language Record* child and parent conferences, reading diaries and samples, and children's own reading diaries and journals.

> I find it fascinating to look back on the records and to see how the children are influenced in their reading by each other, by me, by T.V. – and the way their own preoccupations determine the reading choices they make. For example, there are often references to the way Fayaz is intrigued by complex illustrations. He's far more visually aware than I am! I can use this to draw his attention to the work of illustrators who will extend his interest and sophisticated reading of the images in books and media.

Reading diaries and journals are a valuable means by which teachers can learn about individual reading interests. In Jill's class, as in many classrooms, the journal offers children an opportunity to reflect on the books

A1 Record of discussion between child's parent(s) and class teacher

M. thoroughly enjoys reading; reading every evening. She selects books from school as well as the Public Library. She reads to her mother at the weekend. M. writes a lot too. Writing about special events and outings. She enjoys drawing cards and makes her own books. Loves to paint and draw.
M. is busy all the time helping her mother in the house. She enjoys some television, mainly Indian films.
M. speaks Panjabi at home and is a fluent speaker.
She enjoys maths at home and using text books from the library.

Signed Parent(s)   D.K.K.   Teacher   G.J.V.

READING CONFERENCES-
M. girl Year Three. languages: Panjabi, Hindi, English

A1 Record of discussion between child's parent(s) and class teacher

R. reads all the time at home. Mother feels he has made progress in reading and handwriting. Sometimes R. is helpful at home. He enjoys TV. R. has his own collection of books. He likes to draw & copies writing from books.

Signed Parent(s)   K.K.P.   Teacher   G.J.V.

Date

A2 Record of language/literacy conference with child

I enjoy reading novels.
and playing with my Amstrad
I like school but I'm not too keen
On maths. I like playing football and
looking for old and interesting things.
I like my work this year my
writing and reading and maths have
improved my Hobbies swimming, snooker
football, tennis and horse riding and
I go to a Club called Co-op Club.

Signed Child   R.P.   Teacher   G.J.V.

R. boy Year Three languages: Panjabi, English
(Jill's class)

2 Reading and Writing: diary of observations
(reading and writing in English and/or other community languages)

Date	Reading
	Record observations of the child's development as a reader (inc a range of contexts.

11/9. 'A Witch Got on at Paddington Station' - reads well, fluent, expressive. In book corner for some time selecting book. Re-reads & self corrects if meaning is lost.

19/9. 'A very first poetry book': Reads a selection of poems. Talked about meter & stressing words in italics.

18/12. 'Wake up Dear. It's Christmas' has able to retell story so far, finding relevant quotes. Read confidently, fluently. Good expression - aware that the speech was in rhyme. Could discuss her favourite part.

22/1. 'No Pets Allowed': Was able to retell the story very well. Was confident enough to ask when she didn't understand an aspect of the plot. We re-read that particular chapter. She read this text confidently & fluently.

18/2. Takes many books home - 'into' reading in a big way. Mostly fiction but some information books too.

20/2. 'The Sniff Stories': Found it a rather difficult text to come to grips with initially but after she had grasped the style, she managed quite confidently. Didn't take in all the gist of the story though and needed to follow under lines with index finger.

12/3. 'Alice in Wonderland': Read this very fluently with comprehension. We concentrated on expression & use of italics. Pausing at commas & full stops, considering reading aloud to make it more meaningful for the listener. M. is very taken with this story & borrows it from me regularly (class bk.)

8/4. Small picture bks. — reading aloud to friend

15/4. Very taken with books on Egypt- has taken some home to read.

OBSERVATIONS
M. girl Year Three languages Panjabi, Hindi, English (Jill's class)

A1 Record of discussion between child's parent(s) and class teacher (Handbook pages 12-13)

E's father agrees that E is a very good reader but he thinks he needs more help with the meaning. One hour everyday is spent on religious lessons – reading the Koran. E no longer learns Bengali because he does not settle down – he wants to watch television. E reads letters to his father at home. Sometimes he can't understand them. E's father would like E to have homework. He hopes that E will go on to further education.

Signed Parent(s) __AR.__   Teacher __AL.__

Parent and child conferences, diary of observations, own reading diary and journal.
E. boy Year Four. languages: Sylheti, Bengali, Arabic, English (Alex's class)

A2 Record of language/literacy conference with child I like reading books (Handbook pages 14-15)

My favourite place to read is in a peaceful place, like my bedroom. I would like a library in my house. I can read in English and Bengali and American because it's the same as English. I learned to read by myself with little books, big books and bigger books. I can read Arabic but I can't speak it. I think I need help with my writing

Signed Child ___E H___   Teacher ___AL.___

---

2 Reading and Writing: diary of observations (Handbook pages 40)
(reading and writing in English and/or other community languages)

Date	Reading
	Record observations of the child's development as a reader (including wider experiences of story) across a range of contexts
25/9	"I'm taking Fantastic Mr Fox home. I've read it before but I like it"
28/9	The Great Practical Rumbustification – retold the first story in detail
2/10	On a visit to the Puffin bookshop – "so many good books. I wish I could buy them all" E could discuss his likes and dislikes
5/10	Tilly Owlyglass which he requested after seeing me read it. Listen to him reading this one'
7/10	Professor Branestawm Up the Pole by Norman Hunter (homebook) Could say ferociously - 'a man with anger' "Is it dawn what you call the very first of morning?" – found book with pictures of temples in it on the Egyptian display – looked at the index then contents "Sometimes I see contents first". – "gods – might be temples there"
19/10	Engrossed in comic.
3/11	Read K's chapter book

I've nearly read all of Roald Dahl Books. I like the way he writes his story and the pictures by Quentin Blake. Three of the best books of Roald Dahl is George's Marvellous Medicine and Fantastic Mr Fox and the Twits.
I'm a little sad that Roald Dahl is dead. I like all the Roald Dahl books that I have read and I hope you like them too. I have lots of best books but I think these three are best.

Dear E,
I do like some of Roald Dahl's books but not all of them. I think the 'Minipins' is a good story. I have the book and the tape. Would you like to borrow them? It is sad that Roald Dahl is dead. Perhaps you would be interested in reading about his life in his two autobiographies - 'Boy' and 'Going Solo'.
I would really like to write a book – would you?
          Alex 1/10

I hope we meet some authors at Covent Garden.

Yes I would like to take the Minipins home but we've got a bad tape. I find it hard to find good books for myself. I have been looking for Boy and Going Solo. I have seen Boy but it costs too much to buy.

they have read, and to receive individual guidance about further reading.

At first, the idea of the reading journal was readily taken on by many girls, and probably less so by many of the boys. I'd say the boys tended to use them more like lists and rather competitively in the beginning. But as time goes on, I find there's less of a marked difference in terms of gender. Journals are used for reflecting on the reading they do at home, as well as at school, and all the children regularly take books home. Some children use the journal more frequently, and write at greater length, than others, but it provides a channel of communication, where, individuals can puzzle over questions books raise for them, relate aspects of a story to their own experience, or share their enjoyment of a particular episode, text, or writer. In responding to individual comments and questions, I can recommend other books or authors, read books they're especially excited about to the class, and order books which I know from their responses will sustain and develop their interests. I can put children in touch with others who are into the same titles or share similar interests. This kind of networking is *so* valuable, especially so for boys

DIARY/JOURNAL
S. girl Year Three. languages: Punjabi, Hindi, English (Jill's class)

9.9. Small Monkey Tales: John Cunliffe

9.9. Dirty Beasts: Roald Dahl

10.9 Dirty Beasts & Old Mother Hubbard's Dog: John Yeoman & Quentin Blake

14.9. Witches Four & Stories for Nine Year Olds

17.9. Hairy & Slug

21.9 I have only read a few stories from Funny Stories. I enjoyed reading this book.
I would like to read some more. S.

Which is the best of the stories? Perhaps you'd like to look for a really good longer novel. GN.

22.9 I am reading the Legend of Odysseus. In the first part of the book I have read 4 chapters. The words are hard to pronounce

but I would carry on reading this book because I think it's interesting. S.

23.9 Now I have read 5 chapters. When you read Odysseus to me you read with a lot of expression even though some of the names were difficult to pronounce.
They're hard for me too! It's a great book. I'm really glad you are into it. You seem to like 'Battle with the Gods' particularly. Why is that, do you think? GN.

24.9 The story I liked reading the most was The Battle of the Gods, I think because it was a bit more easier.

25.9. What next? Have you seen The Curse of the Egyptian Mummy? I think you'll enjoy it

29.9. The Curse of the Egyptian Mummy is quite funny. I like the bit where the two were squirting toothpaste everywhere. S. Did you notice who wrote it? GN.

I think. They gain such a lot from talking about the books they have in common and recommending books to each other.

Establishing a core of known and familiar texts with the class group is a key part of Jill's practice, as is helping children to develop their own personal 'core'. She is convinced that for children to be confident readers they need to build a repertoire of texts they both know well and gain a sense of pleasure from reading, alone or with others. Children who are underachieving as readers are likely to need support in this.

B. came to my class with a very limited idea of what reading involved, or what it could offer him. He was convinced it was something he couldn't do, yet should be able to manage. His siblings and peers seemed to read without the same effort. After talking with B. and his mother, we set about concentrating on a core of books which appealed to him and offerred a great deal of support. I don't mean scheme books, but the 'texts that teach' that Margaret Meek talks about. It was important that he wasn't patronised with simplistic texts that undermined his confidence even further. Because we have a wide range of books in the classroom, – poetry, picture books, novels and so on, – the picture books he was introduced to were popular with the other children, too, and they would read with him, with mutual enjoyment. We read the books to him repeatedly at home and at school, put them on tape, encouraged

B's HOME-SCHOOL DIARY
*B. boy Year Four. languages:
English (Jill's class)*

⊕ 'King Rollo & the dishes'
 "   "   " & the balloons' 22.9.
 "   "   " & the search'
 Mum read these to B.
 He read 'King Rollo & the Brush' to me &
 made a good effort at it. He is self-correcting
 as he reads & he is looking for meaning
 – both v. positive points. Get him to re-read
 & take a re-run if it goes wrong. I'm
 encouraging him to have a go at familiar
 books by himself. GN.

⊕ Inky Pinky Ponky –
 B. read the rhymes he could
 I read the rest. VB.

⊕ How's he reading these? At school he's
 managing really well. GN.

⊕ Very confident, "I can read every*
 page of Inky Pinky Ponky"; he told
 us all, and began to read aloud
 a good effort VB.
 * with a little bit of help.

* with a little bit of help.

⊕ I'm really thrilled B. is doing so well.
 He really believes he can read now &
 so do I. A big breakthrough.

 He read 'Lazy Jack' this afternoon
 to me & made a magnificent effort.

⊕ Lazy Jack – Very impressed GN
 with B. Substituting a similar
 word for the one written in
 some cases. Should I ignore
 this or correct him?
 He is also correcting himself
 when he reads the wrong text
 I'm sure he has a very good
 memory though! Anyway, I
 praising him at every
 opportunity. VB.

him to join in and to retell, and make his own versions. Gradually, he took on more of the reading for himself and, we introduced new texts in the same way. He kept a list of the books he knew and liked, which helped foster his independence as a reader. It's taken time, but he has built up a substantial core of books that he now has 'under his belt', and the change in his confidence as a reader and writer is marked.

The social and interactive aspect of reading is given prominence in the reading curriculum offered in both classrooms, accommodating different reading preferences, – such as boys often choosing to work in groups and selecting activities which invite group participation. Both Jill and Alex plan a variety of settings for reading, which both allow for these differences and extend children's shared experience. Contexts include: shared reading in small groups with the teacher; groups working together with multiple copies of the same text; establishing reading partners within the class and with another year group; children reading taped stories together; using the computer in pairs, perhaps for redrafting their writing; and encouraging children to read or talk about their books with their peers and with family members at home.

In her class, Alex varies both the gender composition and the size of the reading groups:

> We've noticed that some girls are less willing to talk as openly about their responses to books in mixed groups, so there's now a balance of single- and mixed-gender groups for shared reading. It alternates, so that children can build their confidence through experience of both. And because girls often seem to participate less in whole-class story sessions, we also plan smaller groups, so they can take a more active role in talking about books.

In addition to extending the range of social contexts for reading, it is also crucial to provide a wide variety of reading-related activities to engage as many children's interest as possible. Book-making is a powerful way for involving both boys and girls in books. When children see themselves and each other as authors, it excites their interest as readers and writers. In both Jill's and Alex's classes, a huge variety of books are made by children, working alone or with others, including ghost stories, class anthologies, information books on the Egyptians and on past topics, poetry collections, and personal accounts. For Jill, book-making is an activity which powerfully connects reading and writing and can be approached at a number of different levels.

> When book-making took off, so did many boys with their writing. It's something they can all do and feel successful at. It's also led to some interesting collaborations – authors and illustrators, authors and editors, writers and translators. I think it's led to many of the girls becoming

more confident in sharing their ideas and skills. The children particularly enjoyed making pop-up books, and this has increased interest in writing generally. They are also more aware of the presentation and style of the books they read. The books they make are very popular, and are read and reread.

Organising 'book events' can be another means of awakening or extending children's interest in books and reading. Recently Alex's class has been involved with dramatising stories in Sylheti and English with the Half Moon Theatre Group, and has also visited Covent Garden to meet the author and illustrator Anthony Browne. Jill is convinced that the established school bookshop plays a significant role in both boys and girls seeing themselves as successful readers in a largely working-class school community.

> Our children now expect to be book owners. They absorb books into their lives as a normal part of their school and home culture. The bookshop has made a real impact on parental interest in their children's reading too, and this has been important for keeping their children's enthusiasm going, I'm sure.

Jill and Alex are both determined to give books and reading a high profile in their classrooms. This high status is communicated to children in the multiplicity of social and learning practices, which all operate together to create rich environments for literacy. Both teachers are committed to recruiting both boys and girls as self-motivated, confident, competent readers of a wide range of texts and genres. They achieve this through a balance of respect for individual interests and an awareness of the power of literacy communities to feed those individual interests and understandings. They are also conscious that children are part of a wider culture which needs to be accommodated within the school context, and connected to school through parental and community involvement, if girls and boys are to understand the relevance and pleasure of reading in their lives.

It is problematic, for several reasons, to try to identify specific teaching approaches in these classrooms that successfully bridge the gender gap in reading. Not all children fall neatly into the gender stereotypes that a superficial attention to test statistics would indicate, and it is important not to perpetuate such stereotypes by seeing children's needs too narrowly and interpreting them only in terms of gender differences. In these classrooms, children are viewed first of all as individuals, and gender divisions have become less marked as a consequence of policies that aim to give all children access to a full range of reading.

The teaching and learning of reading is a complex, layered process, in which gender is one dimension. Although some aspects of the practice

in these classrooms may have a clear role to play in, for instance, supporting boys' reading of fiction, or girls' reading of non-fiction, it is doubtful whether it would be helpful to isolate and describe particular strategies, or to tie up practice into discrete parcels. Attempts to transplant these isolated bits of teaching into other situations, and to apply them without a consideration of the broader context, are likely to be unsatisfactory for teachers and learners alike. The hard lesson that has to be learnt from past attempts to tackle issues of equal opportunities separately from discussions of the rest of classroom practice is that such initiatives cannot truly succeed if they are not part of a general approach to teaching and learning.

As observations of these classrooms have demonstrated, successful practice evolves from a basis of understanding – understanding of the importance that children's interests, tastes, and needs play in their development – and of a context which both supports and extend these interests. This context is achieved by setting up many different kinds of conversations – conversations with the whole group, small group conversations between children – both single-sex and mixed-sex groups, individual conferences between teachers and children, and teachers and parents, and conversations on paper in children's reading journals. Both of these classrooms have established 'literacy communities' in which children's reading is linked to their talk, through the process of continual discussions of texts, and to their writing, which allows them to reflect on texts, and demonstrates the importance of reading in the education of writers. Children's development is apparent not only in their ability to operate as thoughtful and critical readers of a range of texts, but also in their ability to discuss their responses, and in their growing confidence as authors of their own texts.

In these communities, a sensitivity to the ways in which issues of gender and equal opportunities in general can affect children's enjoyment and achievement as readers informs all of the practice in reading. It would be impossible to say whether the generally good level of achievement in both classes, which show less marked a difference between boys and girls than in the studies quoted at the beginning of this article, can be attributed to any particular feature of planning, organisation, or provision. It seems more likely that it reflects the generally high quality of the experiences available to all girls and boys in such classrooms, which set no limits to what they are expected to achieve.

SUE ELLIS
With grateful thanks to Jill Verde and Alex Law and the children they work with. Thanks also to Graham Ford.

Bibliography 1
ACADEMIC BOOKS AND ARTICLES

Adler, Sue. *'Aprons and attitudes: a consideration of feminism in children's books'* in *Equality Matters*, edited by Hilary Claire, Janet Maybin and Joan Swann. Multilingual Matters, 1993

Arnott, M. and Weiner, G. *Gender and the Politics of Schooling* Open University Press, 1987

Askew, Sue and Ross, Carol *Boys Don't Cry. Boys and Sexism in Education.* Open University Press, 1988

Baghban, Monica: *Our Daughter Learns to Read and Write.* Newark, Delaware: International Reading Association, 1984.

Barrs, Myra; Ellis, Sue; Hester, Hilary; Thomas, Anne: *The Primary Language Record: handbook for teachers.* CLPE/ILEA, 1988

Barrs, Myra and Pidgeon, Sue: *'Gender and Reading'.* Language Matters 1986 no.1

Barrs, Myra and Thomas, Anne (eds): *The Reading Book CLPE, 1991.*

Bender-Peterson,S. and Lach, M.: *'Gender Stereotypes in Children's Books: their prevalence and influence on cognitive and affective development'* Gender and Education 1990 vol.2, no.2

Bleich, David. *'Gender interests in reading and language'* in Flynn, Elizabeth A. and Patrocinio P. Schweickart (eds) *Gender and Reading: essays on readers, texts, and contexts.* John Hopkins, 1986

Bristow, Joseph. *Empire boys: adventure in a man's world.* Harper Collins, 1991

Britton, James: *Prospect and Retrospect.* Heinemann. 1982

Butler, Dorothy: *Cushla and her Books.* Hodder & Stoughton. 1979

Chambers, Aidan: *Booktalk.* Bodley Head. 1985

Chodorow, Nancy: *The Reproduction of Mothering.* University of California Press. 1978

Clark, Margaret M.: *Young Fluent Readers.* Heinemann Educational. 1976

Crago, Margaret and Hugh: *Prelude to Literacy.* Illinois University Press, 1983

Davies, Bronwyn. *Frogs and snails and feminist tales: preschool children and gender.* Allen & Unwin, 1989

de Lacoste-Utamsing, C. and Holloway, R.L.: *'Sexual dimorphism in the human corpus callosum'.* Science 216 1982

Feeney, Karen and Hann, Paul: *Survey of Reading Performance in Year 2. Summer 1991.* Lewisham Education. 1991

Flynn, Elizabeth A. and Patrocinio P. Schweickart (eds) *Gender and Reading: essays on readers, texts, and contexts.* John Hopkins, 1986

Foreman E.A. and Cazdan C.B. *'Exploring Vygotskian Perspective in Education, the Cognitive Values of Peer Interaction'* in Wertsch J.V. (Ed) *Culture Communication and Cognition* Routledge and Kegan Paul, 1985

Fox, Carol: *'The Genesis of Argument in Narrative Discourse'.* English in Education 1990. Vol.24,no.1

Fry, Donald :*Children Talk About Books: Seeing Themselves as Readers.* Open University Press, 1985

Gilligan, Carol: *In a Different Voice: Psychological Theory and Women's Development.* Harvard University Press. 1982

Goelman, Hillel, Oberg, Antoinette and Smith, Frank (eds): *Awakening to Literacy* Heinemann Educational, 1984

Graham, Judith: *Pictures on the Page.* NATE, 1991

Grumet, Madeline: *Bitter Milk: Women and Teaching.* University of Mass. Press, 1988

Harding, D.W.: *'Psychological Processes in the Reading of Fiction'.* British Journal of Aesthetics. 1962. Vol.2. April

Harland Linda: *'Why doesn't Johnny skip?'* in *Alice in Genderland* NATE Language and Gender Working Party. National Association for the Teaching of English, 1985

Hassan R.: *The Ontogenesis of Ideology: an interpretation of mother-child talk.* Paper delivered at a conference on Language and Ideology. Sydney University, 1984

Heath, Shirley Brice: *Ways with Words. Language, life and work in communities and classrooms.* Cambridge University Press, 1983

HMI report: *The Teaching and Learning of Reading in Primary Schools.* DES 1990

Hester, Hilary; Ellis, Sue; Barrs, Myra: *Guide to the Primary Learning Record.* CLPE. 1993

Hodgeon, Julia: *A Woman's World? A Report on a project in Cleveland nurseries on sex differentiation in the early years.* Cleveland Education Authority, 1984

Hodgeon, Julia: *'Taking a Look at the Page'.* Language Matters 3, CLPE 1990/1991

Inner London Education Authority: Research and Statistics Branch: *Pupil Achievement in Reading, 1986* *Pupil Achievement in Reading, 1988* *Reading Experience of Pupils: Validation Survey of Reading Scale 2 from the PLR, 1990*

Jantsz, Cindy: *'Year Two Children Writing'* 1993 (Unpublished dissertation)

Jenkinson: *What do Boys and Girls Read?* 1940

Kessler, Suzanne J. and McKenna, Wendy: *Gender:*

an Ethnomethodological Approach. University of Chicago Press. 1985

King, Ronald: *All Things Bright and Beautiful? A sociological study of infants' classrooms.* Wiley, 1978

Kohlberg, Lawrence: *'A cognitive-developmental analysis of children's sex-role concepts and attitudes'* in Maccoby, E.L.E. (ed.): *Development of Sex Differences.* Stanford University Press. 1966

Assessment and Performance Unit: *Language Performance in Schools APU Survey,1984* Leng, I.J.: *Children in the Library.* 1968

Macey, Celia Burgess: *'The Development of Girls' Writing in the Primary School - the influence of gender and genre'.* July 1992 (Unpublished dissertation)

Meek, Margaret: see also Spencer, Margaret

Meek, Margaret: *On Being Literate.* Bodley Head. 1991.

Meek Margaret: *How Texts Teach What Readers Learn* Thimble Press, 1986

Miller, Jane: *Women Writing about Men.* Virago. 1986.

Minns,Hilary: *'Girls Don't Get Holes In Their Clothes'* in *Alice in Genderland.* Language and Gender Working Party, National Association for the Teaching of English, 1985

Minns Hilary: *Read it to me Now!* Virago, 1990

Naidoo, Beverley. *Through whose eyes? Exploring racism: reader, text and context.* Trentham, 1992.

NATE Language and Gender Working Party: *Alice in Genderland,* National Association for the Teaching of English, 1985.

OFSTED: *Boys and English.* Ref.2/93/NS. Department For Education. 1993

Osmont, Pip and Davis, Jenny: *Stop, Look and Listen: an account of girls' and boys'* achievement in reading and mathematics in the primary school. ILEA, 1987

Paley, Vivian: *Boys and Girls. Superheroes in the Doll Corner.* University of Chicago Press. 1984

Payton, Shirley: *Developing Awareness of Print. A Young Child's First Steps Towards Literacy.* University of Birmingham. 1984

Pitcher, E.G. and Schultz: *Boys and Girls at Play.* Bergin and Garvey.1983

Restak, Richard M.: *The Brain has a Mind of its own: Insights from a Practising Neurologist.* Crown Publishing Group, 1991

Reynolds, Kimberley. *Girls only? Gender and popular children's fiction in Britain, 1880-1910.* Harvester Wheatsheaf, 1990

Rosenblatt, Louise M. *The reader, the text, the poem: the transactional theory of the literary work.* Southern Illinois University Press, 1978

Rosenblatt,Louise M. *"What facts does this poem teach you?"* Language Arts 1980

Sarland, Charles: *Young People Reading: Culture and Response.* Open University Press. 1991

Sayers, Janet: *'Psychology and Gender Divisions'* in Weiner, G. and Arnot, M. : *Gender Under Scrutiny.* Hutchinson. 1987

Sex Role Stereotyping and Women's Studies: A Resource Guide for Teachers, Including Suggestions, Units of Study, and Resource Lists Ontario Ministry of Education, 1978

Spencer, M. *'Children's Literature: Mainstream Text or Optional Extra'.* Conference paper given to the Primary English Teaching Association and the English Teaching Association of Australia. Reprinted in Eagleston, R.D.: *English in the Eighties.* Australian Association for the Teaching of English,1983

Strube, P.: *'Narrative in Science Education'.* English in Education. 1990. vol. 24 no.3

Testing 7 year-olds in 1991: results of the National Curriculum Assessments in England, DES, 1991

Thorndike, Robert L.: *A Comparative Study of Children's Reading Interests.* 1941

Tizard, Barbara et al.:*Young Children at School in the Inner City.* LEA, 1988

Vygotsky, Lev: *Mind in Society. Harvard University Press.* 1978

Walkerdine, Valerie: *Schoolgirl Fictions.* Verso, 1990

Walum, L.R.: *The Dynamics of Sex and Gender* (1977) quoted in Delamont, Sara: *Sex Roles and the School.* Methuen. 1980

Wells, Gordon: *The Meaning Makers.* Heinemann.1986

White, Dorothy: *Books Before Five.* Heinemann Educational,1991

White Janet: *'On Literacy and Gender'* in Carter, Ronald (ed) *Knowledge about Language and the Curriculum* Hodder & Stoughton, 1990

Whitehead, Frank et al.: *Children and their Books.* Macmillan Education,1977

Wolf, Shelby Anne and Heath, Shirley Brice: *The Braid of Literature: Children's Worlds of Reading.* Harvard University Press. 1992

Zimet S.G. *Print and Prejudice* Hodder and Stoughton, 1976

Bibliography 2
CHILDREN'S BOOKS

Alphabet, by Fiona Pragoff Gollancz

Animals, by Helen Oxenbury Walker

Asterix books, by Goscinny and Uderzo. Hodder

Avocado Baby, by John Burningham Jonathan Cape. Picture Lions

Baby Goz, by Stephen Weatherill Frances Lincoln

Bear Hunt, by Anthony Browne Hamish Hamilton. Hippo

Bet You Can't, by Penny Dale Walker

The BFG, by Roald Dahl Jonathan Cape. Puffin

Bimwili and the Zimwi, by Verna Aardema Macmillan Picturemac

Charlotte's Web, by E.B. White Hamish Hamilton. Puffin

City, by David Macaulay Collins

Colours, by Jan Pienkowski Heinemann. Picture Puffin

Counting, by Fiona Pragoff Gollancz

The Crimson Tide (Fighting Fantasy Books), by Steve Jackson and Ian Livingstone Puffin

Curtis the Hip-hop Cat, by Gini Wade. Macmillan

Dear Zoo, by Rod Campbell Campbell Blackie. Picture Puffin Dual language editions available from Roy Yates

A Difficult Day, by Eugenie Fernandes. Puffin

Dragonfall Five and the Hijackers, by Brian Earnshaw. O.P.

Dragonfall Five and the Space Cowboys, by Brian Earnshaw. O.P.

Eyewitness Guides Dorling Kindersley

Farmer Duck, by Martin Waddell and Helen Oxenbury Walker. Dual-language editions published by Magi

The Fat Cat, by Jack Kent Picture Puffin

The Flower Fairies, by Cicely Mary Barker. Warne

Friends, by Helen Oxenbury. O.P.

Frog in the Middle, by Susanna Gretz Methuen. *Little Mammoth*

Grandpa's Face, by Eloise Greenfield Hutchinson. O.P.

How Many? by Fiona Pragoff Gollancz

Jamaica Maddah Goose, edited by Louise Bennett Friends of the Jamaica School of Art Association

Jamaica Tag-along, by Juanita Havill. Mammoth

Just Like Jasper, by Nick Butterworth and Mick Inkpen Hodder. Picture Knight

The Lion, the Witch and the Wardrobe, by C.S. Lewis Collins. Lions

Little Monster, by Barrie Wade Deutsch

Look, Touch and Feel with Buster, by Rod Campbell Campbell Books

Marcellus, by Lorraine Simeon. O.P.

Matilda, by Roald Dahl Cape. Puffin

Mom Can Fix It, by Verna Allette Wilkins. Tamarind

Monster Road Builders, by Angela Royston Frances Lincoln

Narnia books, by C.S. Lewis Collins. Lions

Oh Dear, by Rod Campbell Campbell Blackie. Pan Piper

Oh Kojo, How Could You! by Verna Aardema. O.P.

1,2,3, by Rod Campbell Blackie

The Paper Bag Princess, by Robert Munsch Annick Press. Hippo

The Patchwork Quilt, by
Valerie Flournoy and Jerry
Pinkney
Bodley Head. Picture Puffin

Peace at Last, by Jill Murphy
Macmillan. Dual language
editions available from Roy
Yates

Peepo! by Janet and Allan
Ahlberg
Viking. Picture Puffin

Peter Pan, by J.M. Barrie
Several different editions
available, including those
published by Puffin; Orchard;
Pavilion

Piggy Book, by Anthony
Browne
Julia MacRae. Mammoth

Rosie's Walk, by Pat Hutchins
Bodley Head. Julia MacRae.
Picture Puffin

Silly Goose, by Jan Ormerod.
Walker

The Snowman, by Raymond
Briggs. Hamish Hamilton.
Puffin

Snow White and Rose Red, by
the Brothers Grimm
Several versions, e.g. - illustrated by Bernadette Watts.
North/South Books

Spot books, by Eric Hill.
Several titles. Heinemann.
Picture Puffin
Dual language editions of
some titles available from Roy
Yates

Spot Goes to the Farm, by Eric
Hill
Heinemann. Picture Puffin
Dual language edition avail-
able from Roy Yates

Thomas the Tank Engine
books, by Reverend W.
Awdry or Christopher Awdry.
Heinemann

Titch, by Pat Hutchins
Bodley Head. Julia MacRae.
Picture Puffin

The Tough Princess, by Martin
Waddell. Walker

The Way Things Work, by
David Macaulay. Dorling
Kindersley

The Very Hungry Caterpillar,
by Eric Carle. Hamish

Hamilton. Picture Puffin
Dual language editions pub-
lished by Mantra
Watership Down, by Richard
Adams. Puffin

Whatever Next! by Jill
Murphy
Macmillan

Zoo, by Jan Pienkowski
Heinemann. Picture Puffin

COMPUTER PROGRAMS

Nature Park Adventure, by
Simon Hosler. Sherston:
Sherston Software

Pip Goes to the Moon, by
Nepcug group. Newcastle
upon Tyne: Northern
Micromedia

Space Mission Mada, by
Simon Hosler
Sherston: Sherston Software

Through the Dragon's Eye, by
Peter Smith
BBC Enterprises/ Longman
Logotron

Yellow Brick Road, by
Nepcug group. Newcastle
upon Tyne: Northern
Micromedia

ACKNOWLEDGEMENTS

We thank **Doris Anstee** and **Brenda Hockley (CLPE)**
for their work on the manuscript, and **Ann Lazim
(CLPE)** for her work on the bibliographies.

We thank the following schools which have given us
permission to use photographs of their classrooms:
Bannockburn Primary School
Bigland Primary School
Kilmorie Primary School
Pilgrims way Primary School
Richard Atkins Primary School
Sir William Burroughs Primary School
Stebon Primary School

We thank **Bannockburn Primary School** and **Sir
William Burroughs Primary School** for giving permission to use examples of their work in this book.

We thank **Naima, Phil and Rehana Browne, Hazel,
Amy and Alice Polglaze, Phil and Kate Dutton** and
Oliver and Matthew Briggs and **Southwark
Libraries** for giving permission to use their
photographs in this book.

CONTRIBUTORS

Sue Adler has been reading children's books for more than four decades and hopes to do so for another four. A South African, she lives in London where she writes and has part-time jobs, currently with an education trust and a LEA schools'library service.

Michael Annan has taught infants and juniors in Lambeth primary schools for the last five years. Prior to teaching he spent four years working with under 5's in Camden.

Myra Barrs is the director of the Centre for Language in Primary Education, co-author of several of its publications including *The Reading Book* and the *Primary Language Record Handbook* and the editor of *Language Matters*. She is an experienced teacher and publisher, and has written on topics ranging from assessment to the development of the imagination.

Naima Browne has taught nursery and infant aged children for a number of years. She is currently a lecturer in early years education at Goldsmiths' College, University of London. She is particularly interested in equal opportunities in education and her doctorate focussed on the education of working-class infants in 19th century London. She has a 2 year old daughter.

Sue Ellis is deputy drector at the Centre for Language in Primary Education, co-author of *The Primary Language Record Handbook, Patterns of Learning, Guide to the Primary Learning* and contributor to *The Reading Book* and *Language Matters* .

She has worked as a classroom teacher in London and the U.S., an advisory teacher supporting children with reading difficulties and as a reading consultant with *BBC Schools Radio*.

Sara Haynes has worked in Southwark and Tower hamlets for several years. She has worked as an advisory teacher, and most recently as a Section 11 nursery teacher with responsibility for community and parental links.

Julia Hodgeon is a practising early years teacher in the North East of England. She has made extensive studies in the area of literacy and gender.

Hilary Minns is a Lecturer in the Department of Arts Education at the University of Warwick. She was a primary teacher for thirteen years and then headteacher of a Coventry primary school for nine years. She is a former editor of *English in Education*, the journal of the national Association for the Teaching of English.

Pip Osmont has had twenty years experience in Primary Education and has for a long time had an interest in the different responses that girls and boys make to the curriculum. She has, more recently, worked in the field of Traveller Education. This involves working with families who live either on the roadside or on temporary sites, to gain access to schools and most importantly, in the view of the parents, to literacy.

Lissa Paul, an associate professor at the University of New Brunswick, teaches children's literature, literary theory and feminist theory. She writes for *Signal* and other children's literature jounrnals. She has also written support documents for the Ontario and New Brunswick Departments of Education.

Sue Pidgeon lectures in primary education at Goldsmiths' College, University of London and is a member of the literacy group there. She was a primary school teacher in inner London for twelve years and an advisory teacher at CLPE. She has contributed to various CLPE publications.

Valerie Walkerdine is a product of the tripartite system and 1960's expansion of higher education. Originally trained as a primary school teacher, she is now Professor of the Psychology of Communication in the Department of Media and Communication, Goldsmiths' College, University of London. She has undertaken research on gender issues for many years. Her latest book is *Schoolgirl Fiction*, Verso, 1991.